to Marcello
my beloved grandson

First published in Italy in 2004 by
IdeArte srl
Via Regia, 53 - 55049 Viareggio
info@ideabooks.com; www.ideabooks.com

English edition published jointly in Australia in 2006 by IdeArte srl and
The Images Publishing Group Pty Ltd

The Images Publishing Group Pty Ltd
ABN 89 059 734 431
6 Bastow Place, Mulgrave, Victoria 3170, Australia
Tel: +61 3 9561 5544 Fax: +61 3 9561 4860
books@images.com.au; www.imagespublishing.com
The Images Publishing Group Reference Number: 684

National Library of Australia Cataloguing-in-Publication entry:
Gardella, Mariella.
[Ospiti a Capri. English]
Capri style.

ISBN 1 86470 153 6.
ISBN 978 1 86470 153 1.

1. Capri Island (Italy) – Social life and customs.
I. Alvear, Gonzalo de, 1965– . II. Title.
390.094573

Design by Marco de Sensi
Stylist: Mimosa Alvarez de Toledo
Editor Giampaolo Simi
Production by The Graphic Image Studio Pty Ltd, Australia
www.tgis.com.au

Printed by Everbest Printing Co. Ltd. in Hong Kong/China
IMAGES has included on its website a page for special notices in relation to
this and our other publications. Please visit www.imagespublishing.com

I wish to express my profound gratitude to all my friends who helped make this
book possible. I hope they will excuse me for not listing them in alphabetical
order. Some of them would have deserved a star, just as in guidebooks. Heartfelt
thanks to my husband Peter for his patience, undying enthusiasm and valuable
research. Thanks to my children, Giovanni, Margaux and Nick.
I thank Tonino, Renato, Antonio, Mariella and Pietro Esposito and the Hotel
Gatto Bianco. Also, Pinuccia and Riccardo Rocchi of Gemma restaurant.
Marilina, Lina, Alberto, Filippo and Federico of Campanina Gioielli. Silvia and
Salvatore Acunzo of Capri People. Antonio and Iolanda De Gennaro of Foto
Azzurro. Luigi and Ilaria Iacono of the Canzone del Mare. Tonino Cacace of
Capri Palace. Gianfranco Morgano of the Quisisana. Tony Petruzzi of the La
Palma hotel. The following coffee bars: Bar Caso, Il Piccolo Bar, Il Gran Caffè,
Bar Tiberio, Bar da Alberto, Bar della Funicolare and the Dulcis Caffè. Also,
Jessica di Olivetti, Margherita Lembo, Enzo and Pauline Cappa, Tonino and
Gaetano of the Fontelina, the Buca di Bacco, "da Serafina," "da Settanni," the
Buoncore, Elizabeth and Massimo Catuogno, "da Gelsomina la Migliara," Franco
of Villaverde, Ernesto of the Sollievo, Daniela Di Stefano, Iolanda Estranero
Ruocco, Prof. Gerardo Di Meglio, Dr Giacobbe Ruocco, Dr Mariano Bozzaotre,
Allegra Fornaris and Roberto Russo.
Special thanks to Ausilia and Riccardo Esposito of Edizioni La Conchiglia for
their contribution.
Sincere thanks to Piera and Antonio Fontana for their active role from the
beginning in the realisation of this book.

Photography credits:
Gonzalo de Alvear: jacket, 5, 38, 40, 56–61, 74–89, 98, 99, 110–113, 118–123, 126,
127, 138–141, 144, 151, 153, 154, 158, 159, 164, 166, 167
Editor's archives: 39, 42, 45, 54, 70, 73, 142, 143, 155–157, 162, 163
Centro Archivistico Documentale, Capri: 29, 31
Edizioni La Conchiglia: 47
Foto Azzurro: 32, 34
Michael Friedel and Grazia Neri of Milan: 6
Galleria Capricorno: 72
Giovanna Lacatta: 66–69
Massimo Listri: 15, 17, 20, 104–109
James Mortimer: 100–103
Marina Papa: 8, 20, 22, 23, 43, 47, 52, 55, 62–65, 90–95, 124, 128,
132–137, 144–150, 152, 160, 165
Vittorio Pescatori (photo tinted with watercolours): 27
Paolo Signorini, Albergo Caesar Augustus: 129–131
Giovanni Simeone, Sime srl, Treviso: 11, 96
Peter van Schalkwyk: 12, 18, 21, 34, 44, 46, 48–51, 114–117

Mariella Gardella

Capri Style

Photographs by Gonzalo de Alvear

images
Publishing

Contents

My Capri

This book is a compilation, a potpourri of people from former times and current friends. This viewpoint of mine is a bit fragmentary, a bit *quod casu*, with the intention of piquing the reader's interest in Capri and its hospitality. The choice of friends is bound up with the happy times spent with them. And I apologise if I have omitted anyone.

It is curious how the past becomes increasingly more enchanting, and the present more muddled. In any case, I hope I have succeeded in melding so many different moments in my effort to explain what it means to be a guest on Capri.

My connection with the island began in September of 1978 when my husband and I came from Positano to Capri for the day. At the time, we were both working in Milan, and this was our next-to-last day of vacation – but it turned out to be the beginning of our life on Capri. The earliest friends we made were almost all foreigners. My children soon joined us, along with their young friends, all curious about our discovery.

And then there were the natives of Capri – the *capresi* – who are not so easy to get to know. As a matter of fact, they are reserved and perhaps even a bit blasé about the strangers who arrive on their island. I have wonderful memories of those madcap years and the parties and suppers at home or in villas, on the rocky shores or out in a boat, under the blazing sun or at night with a full moon shining. Not much time was left for sleeping.

These days, our life on Capri is different. We spend much of our time on the island, practically the entire year. And so I have rediscovered a great many friends who lead a life akin to our own. So the party goes on, albeit at a less hectic pace. Naturally, we still frequent the Piazzetta on a regular basis.

I continue to write and paint, as does my husband Peter. Then in the winter season there is time for travel and … my grandson Marcello, the most important guest for me on Capri, to whom I dedicate this book.

Capri yesterday

An island has its own laws, different from those of the continent, perhaps owing to the ascetic and anarchic spirit intrinsic to the very idea of island.

For years Capri gave hospitality to Tiberius, because the divinities had prophesied that his life would be safe only if he never left the island. Many other legends speak of him as well.

Svetonius relates that for the emperor, Capri had become a *sedes arcanarun libidinum* or place of secret depravation. It is said that the emperor forced young people of both sexes to make love in his presence. He had special places built, reserved for every sort of vice. Medals were made for distribution that bore a room number on one side and the type of depravity practised there on the other. The great pagan myth surrounding Capri thus begins with Tiberius.

Since that time Capri has been a favourite destination of eccentrics of the international set, a mythical island, a marvellous place removed from the world of everyday mortals and morals, where everything is allowed.

The story of Capri cannot be told without bearing in mind the role played in the early twentieth century by certain personalities belonging to the local dynasties, such as members of the Pagano and Cerio families, who between the two world wars transformed what was largely a primitive island into a cosmopolitan centre.

Giuseppe Pagano, a notary, opened his famous La Palma in 1825. The handsome hotel near the Church of Santo Stefano became a magnet, drawing all the important visitors to Capri in search of lodgings, including German and English artists who painted the magnificent landscape of Monte Solaro from the terraces.

Late in the afternoon the guests would gather in the smoke-filled rooms of nearby Zum Kater Hiddigeigei (a name suggesting life without care), the legendary café run by Donna Lucia Morgano, a great patroness of intellectuals between World Wars I and II. Here fishermen and muleteers found themselves rubbing elbows with German

princes and even the benefactor of the island, arms merchant Friedrich Krupp, the wealthiest and most powerful man in Germany.

Oscar Wilde and Lord Alfred Douglas were among the unwelcome guests of the hotel Quisisana. At the time, Wilde was attempting to leave behind the notoriety that dogged him in England.

The Cerio family, one of Capri's oldest, still today owns the fourteenth-century palazzo that houses the "Centro Caprense" Museum and Library of Ignazio Cerio, father of Edwin, the architect and writer.

When Edwin Cerio became mayor of Capri in 1922, he organised a famous conference on the local landscape, with the aim of protecting the island and its typical architecture. In those same years, architect Carlo Angelo Talamona likewise did his part, interpreting the Mediterranean tradition by mediating it with modernism and the avant-garde, as expressed in a series of projects between Tuoro and Tragara.

The year 1923 marked the death, at slightly more than forty years of age, of Baron Fersen, the leading dandy of Capri between the wars. On Capri, he had built a sumptuous and enigmatic home, Villa Lysis, near the ruins of the palace of Tiberius. Fersen was successor to the symbolist movement, and used his villa as a stage for an inimitable way of life, receiving practically all the Italian and foreign intellectuals of the day, and involving those he was most intimately acquainted with in mysterious pagan rites described with humour by Roger Peyrefitte in his novel *Exile on Capri*, which is the romanticised story of the life of the eccentric baron. In the foreword to the book Jean Cocteau writes: "To be deprived of genius when one dreams of it must be the most terrible torment of all. I have always had a fondness for those creatures unable to create masterpieces, who to make up for it try to become one themselves ..." Like Fersen, other dandies and artists at the turn of the last century lived in sumptuous villas.

In the early years of the twentieth century, the island gave hospitality to persons of culture, including writer Norman Douglas, author of *South Wind*, the Capri novel par excellence that inspired an entire generation. Other figures include D.H. Lawrence, Joseph Conrad and Compton Mackenzie, author of *Vestals of Fire* and *Dangerous Women*, two key novels regarding Capri that with their brilliance and vivacity capture the island's exotic habitués at the beginning of the last century. But perhaps the most important figure was Russia's Maxim Gorky. At that time, Capri was the location of the first school of political propaganda, founded by the Russian Social Democratic Party, which was active right in the middle of the stormiest period in the life of the party that gave rise to the Bolsheviks, from 1908 to 1911.

Those were also the years when the Futurists – Marinetti, Casavola, Cangiullo, Virgilio Marchi and others – discovered the island, and it became their favourite location for staging exhibitions and special events.

The myth of Capri continued throughout the last century; despite the terrible events afflicting much of Europe, the island was both a refuge and adopted home for many intellectuals, artists and writers. They included Longanesi, Monicelli, Soldati, Malaparte, Moravia and Greene and, more recently, Raffaele La Capria and Shirley Hazzard.

Anacapri

For anyone looking for rest and relaxation, there is no better place than Anacapri.

Here, despite real estate development, there are still vast unspoiled areas where the flora thrives in a natural habitat and it is possible to enjoy a brand of peace and quiet hard to find elsewhere. Here, one still breathes the pleasant air of an earlier Capri.

Like two prima donnas, the rivalry between Capri and Anacapri has always existed. At one time, on the Scala Fenicia, there was even a gate dividing Capri from Anacapri that would be closed for the night.

After years of neglect, the Scala Fenicia has now been reopened; at night, illuminated by a cascade of lights, it resembles a string of pearls. Ever since the remote past, there has been a dense network of roads and paths produced by the travels of peasants and hunters on Anacapri.

Customary activities include the tourist walk from the Grotta Azzurra to the Faro (lighthouse), which affords a unique view of the Bay of Naples; the Church of S. Michele with its magnificent majolica floor in pure baroque style; and the house and museum of Axel Munthe.

Off the beaten tourist track are the secluded, lovely villas of celebrities such as Gabrielle Colette and Graham Greene. Most of the latter's novels were written in his refuge, Il Rosaio.

Today Anacapri continues to attract the famous, among them Luca di Montezemolo and Diego Della Valle.

It also offers gracious hospitality thanks to the Capri Palace, the Caesar Augustus and the Hotel Caprile, former residence of the Queen of Sweden.

Capri's guests

Invitations past and present

For a proper discussion of Capri in terms of worldliness, parties, invitations and dinner parties, I think it only right to start from the beginning with the Romans and Emperor Tiberius. Back then, an invitation up to Villa Jovis or down to a grotto for a bacchanal must have been an unforgettable experience, if the cookbook of Apicius or the roguish chronicles of Tacitus and Svetonius are any indication.

Capri was not all that different in the early decades of the last century until the 1930s, owing to the arrival of the first wave of eccentric foreigners. Only parties and scandals involving celebrities punctuated the *dolce far niente* atmosphere. Even in the post-war era and up to the 1970s, party going and party giving were the major occupations on the island. Nowadays, the fondness for entertaining persists, whenever possible with a hint of folly, a bit of snobbery and humour … and boundless zest.

In the early days of the twentieth century, every Sunday without fail the Anglo-American colony would gather at Villa Torricella, the home of Kate and Saidee Walcott-Perry. In *Dangerous Women*, Compton Mackenzie refers to the same couple as Virginia and Maimee Pepworth-Norton, and the house as Villa Amabile.

While the older ladies usually preferred to take a carriage down to Marina Grande, the more energetic among the invited would go by foot down narrow stairs and through fields, vineyards and lemon groves. After tea and sweets – cakes, ice cream or crème de menthe – the guests would take a stroll in the garden, then go back to the terrace, seat themselves in the bamboo chairs and drink unlimited quantities of whisky and soda until sunset. And beyond.

Baron Jacques d'Adelsward Fersen, descendant of the Count Ferson remembered as the lover of Marie Antoinette, was another who chose to spend two decades of his tormented life on Capri at the beginning of the century. Villa Lysis had recently been furnished with electric power, then a newfangled device, so that the whole place blazed with light, while the gardens and stairs to the peristyle were full of Parma violets.

Music, dancing the tarantella, rivers of champagne and poetry – belles lettres were another of Ferson's great passions – and in the Chinese Room, cocaine and opium. One memorable event there was the grand soirée in honour of two duchesses, Elisabeth de Clermont Tonerre and Maria Digramont, née Ruspoli.

The scene that greeted guests at Villa San Michele on the occasion of the party given by Axel Munthe for Marchesa Casati was quite different. The usual furnishings had been replaced with ebony furniture, walls hung with black drapes and carpets of the same colour.

The marchesa herself was dressed all in black and adorned with black pearls and jadeite jewellery. Her hair, alternating between red and green in the past, was now also black. The sole exception was the black servant, 'gilded' from head to toe. Unfortunately, that is all we can say about that sensational evening.

"My name is Fleming, Ian Fleming." This is how we like to imagine the words of the young English writer on his initial appearance at Villa il Fortino in 1938.

Fleming, seduced by the idea that Capri was the most romantic, sophisticated and decadent place in the world, had, together with two friends, just taken lodgings in three rooms of a modest boarding-house whose only desirable feature was the view overlooking the Bay of Naples.

Dressed to the nines, he had a letter of presentation for the owner of the villa, refined American millionairess Mona Williams.

Young Fleming was a lucky man, just as his alter ego James Bond.

He won at backgammon against the cosmopolitan guests of the villa. He remained right where he was at Villa del Fortino for the next month, surrounded by beautiful women and fêted at dinner parties and receptions featuring caviar and champagne. Enormously wealthy, Mona Williams had five husbands, among them Count Eddie Bismarck.

She also had a genuine passion for gardening, which she personally engaged in, wielding a pair of gold pruning shears, a gift from her friend Onassis.

Capri is also associated with fulminant love stories, such as that involving Gloria Magnus. In 1949, during a visit to Capri, she had a fateful encounter with Pietro Cerrotta, a sailor.

They decided to open a restaurant together at Marina Piccola. Success was instant: the menu was perfect, the cuisine excellent. Gloria was attractive, vivacious and brimming with emotion.

Habitually dressed in slacks, she also wore a Carmen Miranda-style turban. At work, she was fond of singing; her speech was a mixture of cockney and snatches of other languages. In the kitchen she would give orders in a strange Italian, so that *frittura di pesce misto* (assorted fried fish) had a way of becoming *fregatura mista* (mixed swindle). The restaurant became a favourite meeting place for vacationing celebrities. Gloria inspired Noel Coward's song "A Bar on the Piccola Marina."

Elsa Maxwell showed up in Capri in the early 1950s. The queen of American gossip had built her fortune on the scandals of the international beau monde.

Attending her parties became a matter of vital importance.

The throngs of partygoers became all but unmanageable with everyone trying to crowd around the hostess for a word with her or even just to be noticed. Nothing escaped her attention, and the day after a party she would remember everything and everybody, without sparing her caustic remarks.

One summer day in 1951, a lively group of friends was gathered around a half-shaded table outside a Marina Grande restaurant. All had close ties with the elderly gentleman seated at the head of the table.

At eighty-three years of age, Norman Douglas still cut a fine figure despite his less-than-perfect health, which forced him to carry a cane, just now resting against a chair holding his hat.

His box of half-smoked cigars sat close at hand on the table.

Seated beside him was agreeable Scotsman Kenneth MacPherson, the bright owner of Villa Tuoro. A key figure in the Anglo-Florentine world, Lord Harold Acton, was also present, with his air of a Chinese mandarin, along with Gracie Fields and Boris Alperovici, with whom she was smitten at the time.

Also in attendance was the eccentric and scandalous writer Nancy Cunard, with her jangling bracelets. Stylish Faith MacKenzie sat at the opposite end of the table, while a detached Graham Greene pursued his own thoughts in silence. Norman Douglas appeared in great good spirits, having just sent back to the kitchen a plate of yellow rice that clashed with his handkerchief of a deeper yellow.

Practically the whole beau monde passed through the Hotel Gatto Bianco in the 1960s and 1970s, among them Lady Kitchen, who had many friends and was one of the most hospitable persons on the island.

All her entertaining was organised by Tonino Esposito, except for her dinner parties held indoors or out in the garden, to which she personally attended. During the same period, many brilliant socialites frequented Capri.

One was Norma Clark, a Norwegian divorcée formerly married to the heir to the Singer sewing machine fortune. Dynamic and *charmante*, she was famous for her fabulous parties. Often not in bed until 5 am, she would be up at 10 the next morning fresh as a daisy and ready for the next round of partying. Another was Laura Gold, a former chorus girl divorced from an American diesel oil tycoon, remarried to an English actor and divorced again. Elegant and cultured, she also drank a bottle of gin a day and threw smashing parties.

Barbara De Witt was a prominent figure on Capri during her summer vacations there in the 1980s and 1990s.

Social life was a serious matter for the sister of photographer Bruce Weber.

She had a way of seeming to know everybody for a lifetime. Her companions included two seamen who would prepare suppers for her on a rocky spur known to them and the ancient Romans.

This suggestive spot and the rather pagan goings-on gave rise to countless stories that may or may not have been entirely true.

In the old town centre of Capri stands the ancient Villa Castello with its incredible hidden garden, owned by the Caravita di Sirignano family. Behind its seven doors is found what is perhaps the island's only authentic salon. The castle is the residence of two brothers, Giuseppe and Alvaro, and their sister

Nila. Their eccentric, formidable parents were the beautiful, enchanting Duchess Anna Grazioli and Francesco Caravita, Prince of Sirignano, great-grandson of the Prince of Salina of *Il Gattopardo* by Tomasi di Lampedusa and an extraordinary bon vivant nicknamed Pupetto.

For three decades beginning in the 1950s, they entertained the most important names in international society and culture, including actresses Joan Crawford and Claudette Colbert, statesman Winston Churchill, and writers Graham Greene and Curzio Malaparte, not to mention beautiful millionairesses Mona Williams and Barbara Hutton, and famous couples such as Maria Callas and Greek shipping magnate Onassis.

So many celebrities have passed through Villa Castello that even the prince admitted that it was impossible to remember them all. These were the years of wonderful parties, and Sirignano was the protagonist of an island that was the unrivalled centre of high society. "I think of Capri," he readily acknowledged, "as my adopted country. I am a good friend of the people of Capri and consider it a privilege to be able to live here. In its own way, it is one of the great moral capitals of the world. Sooner or later, anyone who counts comes to Capri. I have had three children, a great many friends and a great many memories that are, by and large, pleasant ones."

The original and extravagant idea of a regular non-stop Southampton–Capri seaplane flight was his.

The prince's culinary skills were equally impressive, including his spaghetti and zucchini dish invented at the restaurant "da Maria Grazia a Nerano."

Nowadays, behind the seven doors of Villa Castello, his children carry on the family tradition of the art of hospitality with the same enthusiasm and patrician grace that distinguished that of their mother, Princess Anna. Prince Francesco Caravita di Sirignano has left some fragments of his philosophy of life in an autobiography entitled *Memorie di un uomo inutile*. "I am not sure whether it is the odd sort who are attracted to Capri," he wrote, "or people become that way by living here." In confirmation of this, he cited German writer Willie Kluck, who described Capri as "an azure

lunatic asylum where man can find himself."

In the 1990s, a leading figure of the island's society life was a wealthy eccentric American, lovely Katherine Price Mondadori, wife of Leonardo.

Their historic home, known as *lo Studio*, is surrounded by a huge garden of roses, jasmine and bougainvillea, hidden behind walls along Via Tragara.

For many years, this was the meeting place of the cream of the international *Who's Who*.

The simple, but never commonplace, dishes were but one expression of the memorable care lavished on the dinner table. Evenings with Katherine were relaxing in pleasant surroundings that invariably included candlelight and lanterns. When she left the island, the curtain fell on a period the likes of which will not be seen again.

Mariella Motta's love affair with Capri dates back to the time when she used to spend the holidays here with her parents as a little girl. Early on, they stayed at the Hotel La Palma, then at the Quisisana and later in a house with so many rooms that it resembled a hotel. From the early 1990s, Mariella made Capri her permanent home, and she has no regrets about the decision. One feature of the island she is particularly fond of is its natural aspect: the breezes, storms, flowers, sea and especially the sun.

A person who shuns taboos, including the current one banning tobacco, she has learned from the islanders that time is really not of the essence and nothing must be done in haste. In keeping with this philosophy, Mariella loves to cook at her own pace. "Being a perfectionist," she says, "I take pains in preparing my dishes. Of course, that means goodbye to sun and sea! I suppose that's the only thing that keeps me from having guests over every evening."

And it is true that Mariella reserves her charming hospitality for an intimate group of friends. Among the dishes they most delight in is Mariella's celebrated *sartù*, a rice timbale.

Judging from the number of invitations they receive, Antigone and Alfredo Pesce must be counted among the island's best-known inhabitants. Their house may be small, but the atmosphere is immense, secluded as it is in a huge, luxuriant exotic garden near Marina Piccola. Alfredo is a Neapolitan with a great sense of humour – black – and a gift for anecdotes. He took a fancy to Capri some fifty years ago.

And it was here, in August of 1966, that he met lovely Antigone, a South African of Greek origin. They make a delightful anti-conformist couple, sharing a passion for literature and gardening.

They also love cats. Between resident and visiting cats, the felines rarely number less than twenty. Antigone and Alfredo have devised an enviable lifestyle. While she cultivates her cultural interests, he is active in real estate, dedicating odd moments to playing the national lottery. Both endeavours have met with success.

But his consuming interests are fishing and, above all, cooking.

His famously tasty dishes include pasta e fagioli and spolichini. The preferred beverage at the Pesce's dinner table is an excellent red wine, while a well-aged postprandial whisky completes the convivial atmosphere. Sparkling conversation distinguishes memorable evenings at the Pesce home.

Shirley Hazzard is an unusual woman. The well-known Australian writer divides her time between New York, Naples and Capri. Her Capri home is a small apartment with a view.

She is an elegant, romantic type with a style going back to former times. And yet, her interest in today's world is intense. To her, it appears an endless mosaic.

She has a subtle sense of humour that she is fond of displaying with wit and grace. She has frequented Capri for nearly fifty years. She and Graham Greene were famous friends. Her book *Greene on Capri* evokes those times. She still fondly recalls evenings spent together with her husband Francis Steegmuller, Greene and his companion Yvonne Cloetta at their favourite restaurant, "da Gemma."

When she is on the island, it is still possible to encounter her there at her usual table in one corner.

If she is not in the company of friends, she will generally be seen with a good book. Silvio, the pizza chef par excellence, fondly attends to her needs.

Art critic Eugenio Busmanti tells us of the hospitality received in the Capri home of Vittorio Pescatori, photographer, writer and painter.

"I have always attached great importance to the home. In fact, I believe that you can really get to know a person only when you've seen his home. And so I can say that I had the privilege of getting to know Vittorio Pescatori at a rather early stage of our friendship, when I came to Capri to spend several days at his place."

"I crossed the famous Piazzetta and made my way up the steep and narrow streets reserved for pedestrians, and as I did, the countryside spread out in a marvellous way. I reached his house, located in a densely populated area that the people here call the *kasba*, a strictly local term I don't know how old.

Pescatore's dwelling was a regular parallelepiped overlooked by other houses, in a splendid position. Inside, everything was limited to the basics. No frills. It was the complete opposite of the Pompeian baroque decor then all the rage on Capri. I don't believe the word 'minimalist' even existed back then, so I suppose you might call it an example of proto-minimalism."

Maurizio Siniscalco is a Neapolitan aristocrat, true gentleman and *caprese* by choice, with an enthusiasm for antiques. His curiosity and culture have contributed to a successful venture as the co-owner of a gallery of modern art, together with artist Salvino Campos. He lives his life surrounded by beautiful things: antique furniture, gouaches, Neapolitan silver, majolica earthenware and porcelain.

He leads the high life, knowing and frequenting all the island's habitués. What makes his dinner parties so special are the guests, the conversation and the reading of a good book or poem. The setting for all this is a small but evocative terrace covered with a straw awning and always crowded. As the evening draws to an end it is time for the ritual of coffee served from a classic Neapolitan pot … and a little healthy gossip.

Mario Moretti and Renzo Marengo are two intellectuals with a love for Capri. They started coming to the island some three decades ago for brief or not-so-brief periods at their home, called Sopramonte. "We came in on tiptoes, conscious of the fact that the islanders are jealous of traditions that they are reluctant to completely share with outsiders. In the wintertime the island seems to turn inward and, as is the case with any small town, the inhabitants go back to socialising with cliques of family and friends. The outsiders that live here are welcome and well-considered, but rarely enter into the private lives of the natives."

"When summer comes, the houses open up and the social whirl begins again with an endless round of dinners, fancy parties, encounters, exclusions, gossip and love affairs that are either rekindled or blossom, thanks to an island that manages to season everything in life with passion."

Hospitality, according to Guia Sospisio, is "a simple little word … but grand. Not because it is necessary to entertain in a grandiose manner, but because of what it represents: communication, friendship, warmth." Hospitality is second nature to most people in Southern Italy, a spontaneous trait difficult, if not impossible, to teach. "I am a woman of the South," Guia explains, "and on Capri I rediscover all the strength of my roots. So when I open my door to friends and their guests, my paramount desire is to make them all feel at home. The rest comes naturally."

"In Italian," says Capri enthusiast Roberto Ciancio, "the meaning of the word *ospite* is complete, since it is the same for both 'host' and 'guest.' Capri receives an ordinary tourist with the same gracious manners as it receives an aristocrat or sophisticated traveller. It never denies the island's charm and incomparable beauty to anyone. It has been a delighted and stimulating host to those who have spent their happiest moments here – and will be the same for those who have yet to discover it. Just think in how many homes around the world Capri is a guest of honour in the form of a keepsake photo, painting, souvenir or picture postcard … or even a hidden love letter."

Capri's culture of hospitality

Artists, cultivated Grand Tour travellers, members of the most aristocratic families and the founders of industrial dynasties were the discoverers of modern Capri. They are the ones who made it a myth. Thus it came about, from one century to the next, that certain Capri families in turn founded real dynasties under the banner of the cult of receiving visitors. Over time, the cult has developed into an art – the art of sublime hospitality.

Hotel La Palma

Just a few steps from the Piazzetta, the historic palm from which the hotel takes its name stands out, much as it appears in Hans Christian Andersen's pen and ink drawing. It was notary Pagano who, in 1822, converted part of his home into an inn to accommodate Grand Tour travellers, thus marking the beginning of the story of hospitality on the island.

A few years later, in 1826, a guest staying at the inn, August Kopisch, discovered the entrance to the Grotta Azzurra. After

writing a report on the discovery in the hotel guest book, he announced the news to the rest of the world.

The hotel's terraces gradually became a privileged observatory of artists, especially German artists, including painters, composers such as Mendelssohn and poet Joseph Victor Scheffel, who completed his long poem, "The Trumpeter of Sakkingend" at the hotel. The guests took their meals *en plen air* and their coffee under the shade of the pergola. Before long, the hotel's success prompted the first of several remodelling projects. Around the turn of the century, La Palma numbered among its guests non-conformist Victorians, aesthetes modelled on D'Annunzio, the idle rich, and Russian exiles attracted by the figure of Maxim Gorky. Many of them returned the hospitality by decorating the walls or donating a work. One result was a singularly well-stocked library, as reported by Allers the painter, himself the author of a delightful set of drawings portraying a number of the hotel's guests. In later years, the great Caruso left a trace of his stay by blackening a plate with smoke from a candle and drawing a caricature of himself on it with a toothpick. The early twentieth century was the heyday of the dandies, Dadaists and Futurists. After World War II, many other personalities stayed at the former inn. Foremost among them was the Prince of Capri par excellence, Francesco Caravita di Sirignano, who spent several seasons here during the final years of his brilliant life. This is where he chose to celebrate his eightieth birthday with a memorable banquet. The Countess Madeleine Pozzo di Borgo of an old aristocratic Corsican family was another assiduous presence in post-war Capri, as was Princess Giovannona Pignatelli Cortez d'Aragona. It was here that Lina Wertmuller inaugurated her successful film festival, *Capri Hollywood*. Rede Globo magnate Ireneo Marinho is remembered for the dozens of green and yellow Brazilian flags he hung on the front of the hotel to mark his country's victory in the final game of the 1994 World Football Championship. There is a special quality that La Palma has maintained throughout its long history, and still does today, thanks to Toni Petruzzi – a simple form of hospitality, never pretentious, which is what makes the style great. The style of Capri.

The Morgano family

Capri at the turn of the twentieth century was divided into two separate worlds: that of the resident foreigners and that of the native population. Today's Caffè Morgano, once owned by Giuseppe and Lucia Morgano, was founded in 1889. Until

1922, it was the hub of the social life of the island's foreign community. In those days it was called Zum Kater or Hiddigeigei, from the name of the cat mentioned in Joseph Schettel's poem "The Trumpeter of Sakkingend." The celebrated coffee shop, now surrounded by myth, was originally mainly a general store where foreigners did their everyday shopping, ranging from tea to whiskey and soap. It even functioned as a currency exchange. The foreign community tended to subdivide along national lines. The Russians, for example, would gather in one corner for games of chess or animated debates over the fate of the Revolution. The Germans instead are remembered for celebrating the birthday of Kaiser Wilhelm II each January with memorable festivities. After World War I, what was left of the foreign colony continued to meet here, as was the case with the leading characters of Compton MacKenzie's *Dangerous Women*. Painter and writer Alberto Savino thus described the abiding sprit of the place: "The Morgano or Hiddigeigei is the most hospitable and convivial café in the world: it is a café *a table d'hôte*."

Upon the demise of Giuseppe Morgano, his widow sold the business. However, the ever-growing Morgano dynasty has continued right up to the present in a related line that likewise puts a premium on hospitality. The children and grandchildren of Don Giuseppe are credited with the success of some of Capri's most renowned hotels, including the Pazziella, La Scalinatella and the more recent Casa Morgano and La Flora, as well as the Quisisana, which Mario and Pina Morgano have returned to its rightful place among the world's finest hotels and key factor in the social life of Capri.

The Esposito family

In the immediate aftermath of World War II, two brothers, Giovanni and Tonino Esposito, founded a restaurant called the Gatto Bianco, which later also became a hotel. Early on, the establishment became the most defiant emblem of the *dolce vita* of Capri. In his *Breviario di Capri*, Amedeo Maturi portrays Giovanni as the modern incarnation of the Roman cupbearer Hypathos, ever ready to satisfy the culinary whims of the emperor Tiberius. In the 1950s and 1960s, the hotel's hospitality was synonymous with a unique, fantastic theatricality, where joie de vivre took centre stage.

For at least a few hours, every customer could cast himself in a leading role in the splendid comedy. Even today, one can experience this magnificent illusion in the grand halls with their majolica floors.

Canzone del Mare

In the 1950s, famous English singer and actress Gracie Fields teamed up with her husband, director Monty Banks (Mario Bianchi), to create what would become Capri's best-known beachfront establishment, the Canzone del Mare, now owned by Luigi Iacono. It is a stylish, peaceful spot surrounded by the enchanting natural beauty of Marina Piccola. Its seawater swimming pool was the island's first. The cuisine recalls the high standards of the past. When night falls, the partying begins under the stars by candlelight with a background of illuminated cliffs. While the society dinner parties that have been held here are too numerous to mention in detail, one of the most memorable has gone down in local history as "the party of princes." The occasion was the birthday celebration in honour of Prince Ruspoli, organised by Hugo Windisch Graetz. All the crowned heads of Europe participated. The annual gala of the Capri Yacht Club is a regular event at the Canzone del Mare. The memorable 2004 gala celebrated theatrical costumer Tirelli Costumi and its forty years of activity. The grand evening celebration captured the essence of what it means to be a guest on Capri.

Da Gemma

In the 1930s, Gemma and her husband Raffaele, better known as *'u chef*, opened a small restaurant with a few tables on a terrace overlooking the heart of the island. If the menu was limited, the food was authentic.

Times were not easy, what with the war and then the difficult years of reconstruction, but Gemma always looked ahead, confident that Capri's allure would reward her efforts. The instinctive commitment led her to create a business destined to become part of the island's history. All sorts of celebrities have patronised the restaurant, while the present proprietors, Pinuccia and Riccardo Rocchi now greet the children and grandchildren of the most faithful early customers. Hundreds of snapshots of customers line the walls and ceiling, along with one of Gemma wearing her red apron and unaffected smile. It would not be overstating the case to say that people come here not only to dine, but also to take a sentimental journey back to an earlier Capri. One can almost hear the echoes of the voices and hearty laughter of the past, and imagine the attire and extravagant coiffures of the ladies. We can almost feel Gemma's affectionate hand touch our shoulder: "*Allora, signo'* – what will it be this evening?"

La Capannina

The history of one of Capri's most characteristic restaurants goes back to the 1930s, initially in the form of a trattoria a few steps from the square. La Capannina was an instant success with writers Norman Douglas and Curzio Malaparte, and other intellectuals who enjoyed rubbing elbows with local customers, including Marina Grande boatmen, or *pallonisti*, as they were then called. The simple fare was based on local products, including unbottled wine. In those days, the only wine sold on Capri was local, until proprietor Francesco De Angelis began special-ordering small flasks (*pulcianelle*) of sweetish wine from Orvieto for Douglas. Bringing the wine to the Scotsman's table was one of the first tasks De Angelis assigned to young Antonio, who as a child enjoyed roaming around the tables of his father's restaurant.

In the early 1960s, the De Angelis family purchased a small rustic place in the middle of Via Le Botteghe. In a garden hidden from the street, grapevines climbed chestnut posts. The ground was unpaved. The task of choosing a name for the new restaurant fell to the illustrious clientele. 'Capannina' won out, in keeping with the rustic atmosphere. Now, over three decades later, a glass roof covers the garden. But judging from the habits of steady customers, including those who are on Capri only once a year, dropping in on Antonio and Aurelia is like going back home again and finding it just as before.

Il Piccolo Bar

"The Piccolo Bar is much more than just another coffee bar. It's a piece of history, and not only of Capri. It is, without a doubt, one of the most photographed subjects anywhere in the world."

These are the opening words of Raffaele Vuotto, who back in the late 1930s was the only one on the island who made ice cream and whipped cream. "I'd bought a very expensive machine for making ice cream," he goes on, "but my lemon sherbet was a real success. Then we began to put tables outside. And that's how the myth of the Piazzetta was born."

Raffaele Vuotto recalls when writers used to meet here, such as Curzio Malaparte ("an extraordinary gift of the gab") and Norman Douglas ("a real dandy").

"The English used to come, the Germans and also the Russians, who would organise chess tournaments at the Zum Kater with the best players of the time. And in the meantime, they were laying the groundwork for the Revolution."

La Campanina

For the many aficionados of Capri, a cup of coffee or aperitif at Alberto and Lina's Campanina marks the true moment of their return to the island. It is the their first chance to say hello to old friends after the winter hiatus.

It also represents their first, invariably pleasant encounter with the real natives of Capri, well versed in the art of hospitality, who fill them in on the latest local news or the restaurant of the moment. It is hard for the ladies to resist the temptation of taking at least a quick look at the rich displays of fine jewellery in the shop windows.

Foto Azzurro

The story of this family business begins in 1953. Newlyweds Tonino De Gennaro and Iolanda Gagliardi had recently opened a photography shop on the azure island. He did the photography, while she worked behind the counter of the little shop on Via Vittorio Emanuele, the Foto Azzurro. Tonino was good at his job, but perhaps his likeable personality counted at least as much as his skill with a camera. He had a winning smile that reminded people of Jack Lemmon. This was the key to his swift rise as one of the island's most famous photographers, but with a style that had nothing in common with paparazzi aggressively pursuing their prey. Instead, Tonino was amiable enough to become friends with many celebrities. His first special customer was the most admired First Lady in the world, Jacqueline Kennedy. With her unaffected manner and natural elegance, discreet Jacqueline not only chose Tonino as her personal photographer, but also was often a guest of the De Gennaro family, to, among other things, enjoy homemade *tagliatelle e fagioli*. The friendship with Jacqueline Kennedy was the first of many involving important people, such as B.B. or Brigitte Bardot, who was likewise fond of Jolanda's cooking.

Alberto Moravia and famous French cardiologist Carpentier were regular guests at the De Gennaro home. Today, half a century later, the business has grown and consolidated thanks to the help of their five children and the launching of a line of eyeglasses.

La Fontelina

As a way of talking about La Fontelina, Tonino and Gaetano cite a few passages from a letter written by a guest, Giuseppe Aprea. "A house suspended in the blue. A soft bed of rock washed by the sea. A dream? Even more.

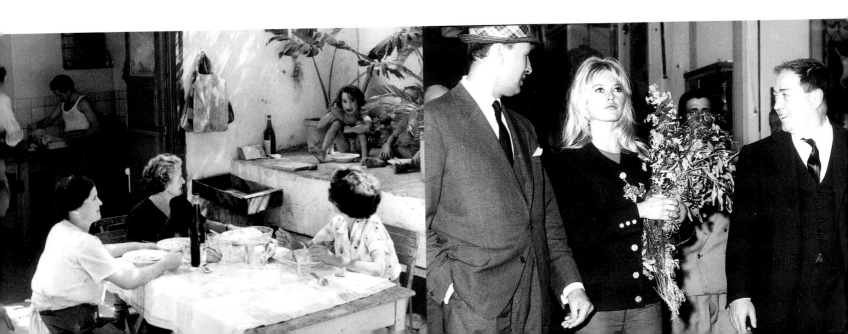

Have you ever experienced the thrill of a view from the marvellous belvedere of Tragara? Look down, where the tidewater that caresses the cliffs meets the stony body of the island. Right there where, like lazy seagulls, white cushions can barely be made out here and there. Now Pablo Neruda's *Isla de Rocha* is all around you, in the flowery walls, in the myrtle, in the shady carob trees. His verses carved in marble mark the path to take along the narrow winding road leading down to the sea and silence. Down there is where you will find La Fontelina … It is the place, on the edge of arid land and salt water, where the women of Capri once ret flax (*lino*). Hence the name *fonte del lino*. Here you must quietly sip a glass of cool Fiano or a good Aglianico: in your heart you will hear the voice of Chile's great poet: 'Wine the colour of day, wine the colour of night, wine with feet of purple, or blood of topaz, wine, starry son of the earth … ' And if the sunset catches you happy down there, do not be too surprised. Life awaits you on a soft bed of rock. Where that house is suspended in the blue."

Caesar Augustus

Today the Signorini family is the jealous custodian of a marvellous residence on Anacapri that possesses the 'essence of the villa' in its very being, owing to both history and tradition. It stands on an exceedingly beautiful spot, beloved ever since Roman times. Already in 1850 the dwelling was famous with the name of Villa Bitter, the private residence of a moneyed German who was among the first foreigners to happily settle on the island. In the early twentieth century, Russian Prince Emmanuel Bulhak decided to move to Italy, choosing this very place to make his home. Thanks to his efforts, for more than three decades it was considered to be one of the finest patrician residences on the island. He was also responsible for placing the statue of the Emperor Caesar Augustus here, where even today the imposing figure seems to greet guests with a welcoming gesture.

While each room in the villa has its own distinctive features, they all share the same spectacular view. Caesar Augustus remains a truly 'exclusive residence.'

Il Capri Palace

The story of the Capri Palace is the story of the Cacace family and the hospitality of Anacapri – and, at the same time, a dream come true. In the early 1960s, at the foot of the hill named Monte Solaro, in the most untamed and fascinating part of the island,

the Europa Palace Hotel made its appearance amid vineyards and citrus groves. Today's guests still feel right at home there, thanks to the courteous, warm reception of Mario, his wife Rita and son Tonino, who will carry on the family tradition.

In addition to following in his father's large footsteps with commitment and determination, it will be Tonino's responsibility to meet the challenge of transforming the Europa Palace Hotel into a luxury hotel, the Capri Palace Hotel & Spa.

Following extensive restyling along classic Mediterranean lines, the hotel has been admitted to the select group of "The Leading Small Hotels of the World."

Today it a favourite destination of famous names in the world of politics, culture and entertainment. The Capri Beauty Farm, founded by Tonino, opened more than a decade ago. The renowned fitness centre combines hospitality and cordiality with both modern and traditional medicine.

Roberto Russo

Well-known Capri entrepreneur Roberto Russo is capable of summing up the island's hospitality in a few words.

"Two thousand years ago, Capri was a great favourite with the emperor Tiberius, to the point of almost making it a second capital city. Ever since, hospitality on the island has evolved and become more refined, while continuing to distinguish itself for its unmistakable style.

On Capri everybody sees and is seen, but at the same time the discretion and respect that the people of Capri accord to each guest has no equal anywhere in the world. The inappropriate curiosity sometimes reserved for celebrities is unknown to the island. It's not unusual to see a native giving a great writer directions to Piazzetta di Tragara or showing a famous actor the way to Villa Jovis, done in the customary unaffected, courteous manner.

The people of Capri don't care about spotting the famous or hunting autographs. They shun being immortalised with celebrities. Here a former empress or a head of state can enjoy a vacation as ordinary tourists. Hospitality is in the very air of our island."

The famous "Piazzetta"

The anteroom of Capri and obligatory first stop for incoming guests is the Piazzetta or *chiazza*, as the locals call it. It is the island's focal point and outdoor living room, a place that mixes the sacred and profane, providing a meeting place for society. Arriving here for the first time from Marina Grande, one discovers a sort of tiny open-air theatre wedged between the stairs leading up to the baroque church and medieval bell-tower – Norman Douglas used to call it the noisiest in Southern Italy – newsstand, town hall, tiny tourist office and Capri's oldest boutiques.

The Piazzetta as we know it today came into existence in 1938 when a young islander, Raffaele Vuotto, following long negotiations with the local authorities, succeeded in obtaining permission to open the Piccolo Bar, including the placing of tables outside. Back then, the space was free of everything but car and carriage traffic, whereas today it is occupied by a total of four cafés: the Piccolo Bar favoured by the local populace, the Gran Caffè with a view of the bell-tower (but here the tolling of the hours has relatively slight importance), Bar Tiberio catering to newcomers, and Bar Caso with its habitués, seemingly there to prop up the bell-tower.

The fact is that people come to Capri for more than just the natural beauty. They want to be players in the daily drama, to see and be seen. This is what the Piazzetta is really all about. It is here that the evening begins with the ritual, "We'll see you later at … "

La casa sotto Tiberio

"This evening we are going to Mariella and Peter's." This is how an invitation is spoken of on Capri. Peter and I have been on the island for more than thirty years. Like many others before us, we arrived one day and never really left again. On Capri in the 1970s there was a certain atmosphere of 'letting go,' an international flavour that foreigners loved back then, and still do. It goes without saying that life has changed, everywhere and for everybody. Norman Parkinson, the fashion photographer and portraitist of the Royal Family of England, back after a fifty-year absence, often remarked that the island was the same as before, only the people had changed a great deal. That notwithstanding, Capri basically remains at least one remove from the rest of the world. Peter and I spend most of the year here. I suppose we deserve some credit if our grandson Marcello, a three-year-old very dear to us, has already learned to appreciate the air you breathe here. I have two children, Giovanni, a writer and poet, and Margaux, a journalist. She and her husband Nick Ferrand, an English company director, have left London to live on Capri. In the beginning, our house was quite different: there were no columns and plants were lacking, with the exception of a solitary suffering olive. The house is small, meaning that during the warm summer months the two terraces serve as a living room and dining room, shaded by huge oriental awnings. In the summertime we spend much of our time at home writing or painting, or else away visiting friends. I immensely enjoy inviting people over for dinner, tea or supper; six or eight people is an ideal number. I adore setting the table differently each time. Sometimes I use a beautiful white damask linen tablecloth and others just plain straw placemats. I also like using English wooden coasters lacquered black and gold, and even unmatched plates. My favourite dinnerware is white and blue ceramics from Vietri. Most of all, I like setting with lots of glasses, even though afterwards I stay up

half the night washing them! The menu varies, ranging from *fusilli* with zucchini to the classic spaghetti with tomato sauce and basil, and delicious little croquettes of aubergines with rice, chicken and curry powder. Then there is baba au rhum, the rum-flavoured sponge cake, or lemon delights. One mustn't overlook the importance of the appetisers. They must absolutely include black and green olives from Gaeta, bite-size mozzarella, salami and sausages, and be accompanied by an excellent iced wine. Peter claims that my virtuosity in the kitchen comes from the pan and that much hinges on my mood at the time, the type of guests,

the sea waves, the moon. And so I indulge my whims at table, always by candlelight in the evening. The truth is, I'm incapable of doing the same thing the same way twice in a row. One thing I loved about New York was the huge floral arrangements in the lobbies of the grand hotels. Sometimes I do the same here; it's a luxury I allow myself just for the *plaisir des yeux*. Summers are so much fun living the high life, but when September rolls around I heave a sigh of relief … and life goes back to small-town living where one learns to attach the proper importance, meaning not very much, to the sense of time.

Pollo al curry con riso pilaf

Summer. There is no cause to marvel at the idea of using curry powder in the summertime. In any warm-weather country you will always find a lot of pepper being used, a lot of spices. They aid digestion, make one's blood pressure rise like a tonic, and preserve foods from spoilage.

Sauce: 1 onion, 100 g curry powder (the curry powder of Cross and Blackwell of London is very good), 1 apple cut up into small pieces, ½ litre fresh cream, butter and salt.

Chop onion and sauté. Add the small pieces of apple and curry powder. Brown for 5 or 6 minutes, then add fresh cream. Force the result through a drum sieve to make the sauce smooth, to be poured hot over diced chicken. Flour diced chicken breasts on both sides and fry in butter and olive oil. Serve with pilaf.

Begin the meal with a refreshing dish of melon and prosciutto, and end it with mulberry ice cream. For wine, either Lacryma Christi or Greco di Tufo. As an aperitif, Bellini.

Delizie al limone

Puff pastry: 250 g water, 100 g butter, 5 g salt, 150 g flour, 5 eggs, rind of one lemon.

Lemon creme: 500 g lemon confectionery creme, 250 g whipped cream.

Heat a pot of water with salt, butter and lemon rind.

When the water comes to a boil, remove lemon rind and add flour.

Stir over heat for approximately 5 minutes until mixture stiffens.

Remove from burner and beat in eggs one at a time.

Using a confectioner's bag, form little balls on a greased oven tray and bake for 30 minutes at 180 °C.

Fill the shells with lemon creme.

La Caterola

A splendid wood thick with Mediterranean vegetation, just below Villa Jovis, surrounds Villa Caterola. The flora includes pine, ilex, oak, cypress, lentisk, arbutus and dwarf palms planted last century by writer Norman Douglas. The many small paths invite one to take a pleasant stroll in the park, perhaps at sunset.

Luncheon invitations from the Caprotti family are a delight. Ida and Guido, two exceptional hosts, are both natives of Milan born to old Lombardy families; they possess a rare talent for spontaneous, natural hospitality. To be their guests in the summertime means relaxing at the edge of a swimming pool, atop a cliff falling vertically to the sea and with a view of the bay that includes Ischia and Procida in the distance. Another possibility is to first take it easy in a comfortable hammock in the shade of venerable pines with a glass of good chilled white wine offered by Guido, conversing amiably with cultivated and brilliant friends before proceeding to a table decorated in turquoise and aquamarine tones, the favourite colours of the hostess. Today the menu includes a potato dish called *gattò*, *scapece* zucchini, sea robin *all'acqua pazza* with mulberry and almond ice cream to top it off.

Pastiera

Filling: 500 g wheat, 500 g ricotta, 350 g sugar, 250 g skinned almonds, 7 eggs, candied fruit as desired, 1 lemon, 1 orange.

Short pastry: 3 eggs, 1 lemon, 100 g sugar, 250 g flour, 150 g butter.

Spread the flour with a well in the centre, add eggs and grated lemon, then butter and sugar mixed separately. Knead swiftly until a consistent mix is obtained and refrigerate for 2 hours.

To make filling, force the ricotta through a sieve, combine with sugar and eggs. Mix well before adding chopped almonds and candied fruit, grated orange and lemon. Mix well. Roll out dough and add filling. Finish the cake with strips of short pastry.

Place on buttered tin and bake for 40 minutes at 180 °C.

Gattò

1 kg potatoes, 200 g butter, 500 g mozzarella, 300 g mortadella, 6 eggs, 200 g parmesan, breadcrumbs and salt as desired.

Boil potatoes, mash and add butter. Thoroughly mix before adding eggs and salt, then thoroughly mix again before adding mozzarella and mortadella cut into pieces, and parmesan. Butter the baking tin and add breadcrumbs. Place the mixture on the tin and sprinkle again with breadcrumbs. Place in heated oven and bake for at least 1 hour at 200 °C. Serve piping hot.

Sea robin or gurnard with tomatoes

Sea robin, small tomatoes, parsley, garlic, olive oil, pepper or hot pepper.

Cover bottom of shallow pot with olive oil and place sea robin in the pot. Cover sea robin with chopped tomatoes, garlic and parsley.

Cover pot and cook for about 25 minutes. Remove sea robin and continue cooking sauce briefly to thicken. Serve with toasted bread.

La Fiorada

She says it is impossible to imagine what her life would be like without La Fiorada, her Capri home. Perhaps this is what prompted Fiorella Buonomo, together with her husband Adalberto, to bring the yellow of the sun and blue of the sea around Capri inside the villa itself, where all is light and colour.

"Capri is my home and my home is Capri," she continues. "It's the sun setting behind Ischia in the distance that makes me a gift of its last gilded rays; it's the sea extending beyond the lemons and my roses. I experience my home in a visceral way that is as all-absorbing as it is stimulating."

La Fiorada rises along the old road leading to Villa Jovis, the residence of Emperor Tiberius. In this corner of Capri, immersed in an unspoilt nature both wild and colourful, the pungent smell of the sea mingles with the milder fragrance of the countryside.

"Capri," says Fiorella, "is at one with the joy of entertaining all my many friends." When we ask her to reveal the secrets of her hospitality, this is her reply: "First and foremost, elegance and sobriety. The distinctive touch of a supper need be nothing more than the sound of a guitar or a plate of spaghetti with *piennolo* tomatoes, the kind you normally find hung outside greengroceries."

"Capri," she concludes, "also means rediscovering serenity in a landscape of intense but reassuring colours. A unique, irreplaceable spot."

Spaghetti ai pomodorini del piennolo (4 servings)

400 g spaghetti made from durum wheat, approximately 250 g tomatoes (the *piennolo* type is ideal), 1 hot pepper, extra virgin olive oil, chopped parsley, 5 crushed garlic cloves, salt.

Brown garlic and hot pepper in large skillet, using plenty of olive oil.

Slice tomatoes in half and place beside each other face down. Add salt and cook at high temperature for 6 or 7 minutes. Use a wooden spoon to stir tomatoes if necessary.

Pour spaghetti cooked 'al dente' directly into the skillet with the burner turned off. Stir gently and place in serving dish, adding a good amount of chopped parsley.

La Micella

La Micella is the Capri home of Graziella De Simone.

"I have a great fondness for Capri," she relates. "In recent years I find that I prefer the winter months to the summertime because that is when the islanders regain the island, the piazza and coffee bars, whereas in the summer a multitude of tourists and holiday-makers invade the place, as is true all over the world nowadays … Livio De Simone, my husband, was also in love with Capri, so naturally we used to come here often. We have had this house since the 1960s, which is the reason why I have remained on the island. I consider it my true home. It's where I have my friends. And my dogs live in freedom, just like me."

"I usually prefer to have guests over in the evening for dinner, no matter how many or few. In the summertime we stay outside under the shade of the straw roof, while in the winter we sit around the low table by the hearth."

"I adore seafood, but not the kind raised on fish farms. I like it baked *all'acqua pazza* or with potatoes spread out so as to cover the pan. All it takes is a little garlic, white wine, parsley, salt, white pepper and peeled *piennolo* tomatoes. Extra virgin olive oil is indispensable. A good rule of thumb is to do the cooking in an earthenware pot."

Pesce all'acqua pazza

1 fish (preferably *pezzornia*), ½ glass lukewarm water, extra virgin olive oil, chopped parsley, piennolo tomatoes, garlic, white pepper, salt, ½ glass white wine.

Place all ingredients in a large pan. Put half the peeled tomatoes through a blender, halving or quartering the rest. Fill the belly of the fish with salt. Bake at low temperature, turning the fish over from time to time.

Calamaro imbottito

1 large squid (minimum weight 700/800 g), 8 langoustines, rice (preferably the *carnaroli* type). *Place uncooked rice in a bowl. Shell the langoustines, cut them up together with the squid tentacles and add to rice. Add and mix olive oil, white wine, salt and white pepper. Fill the body of the squid with the rice mixture and close with a skewer. Place in casserole with ½ glass water, white wine and olive oil. Bake in hot oven for about 30 minutes.*

Villa Tuoro

Today Villa Tuoro is the residence of Semiramis Zorlu and her husband John Lee. The painter and sculptress spends part of the year in Capri and the remainder in Paris and Switzerland.

In addition to her strikingly fair complexion and blonde hair, Semiramis is an impeccably chic woman. She is also a witty personality passionately devoted to her art. She is blessed with energy; not a day goes by without her heading down to the beach in the late afternoon for a swim in the sea off the island she considers her own.

John is a singularly well-mannered and intelligent man with a well-developed sense of English humour. Their terrace dinner parties are pleasant, relaxing events with a style and distinction rarely seen these days. This particular evening a full moon adds its light to the candles. So pleasant is the conversation that as the evening draws to a close we experience a pang of regret for an experience likely never to be repeated. Semiramis confesses that she was taken with the charm of the property the moment she began the climb the cypress-lined stairs leading to the main gate.

This love at first sight was obvious enough that the owner at the time, Kenneth McPherson, was convinced that at last he had found the right person to care for a place with such a special history and so much charm.

Villa Tuoro is in fact forever linked to the figure of Scots writer Norman Douglas, who lived here from the post-war period up until the time of his death in 1952.

During those years, the house was the property of his great friend McPherson, also a writer, whose work included scripts. McPherson went on living here until 1957 together with Islay Bowe-Lyons, a cousin of the Queen Mother of

England. Bowe-Lyons personally attended to the landscaping of the garden. On the ground floor, in the room where Douglas used to work, his writing desk and books are still in place. The windows here all look onto the garden, while as one mounts the stairs to the main floor, a panorama appears that stretches from Marina Piccola to the Certosa, and from Monte Solaro all the way to Ischia.

Recent work has resulted in the addition of a splendid roof terrace and the knocking down of a few partition walls, but the house's original style has been scrupulously preserved, including the terracotta floors and chestnut casings.

Villa Narcissus

Each year at the beginning of summer, the vivacious, witty and original lady of Villa Narcissus returns from her extended travels to open her island home. Her appearance coincides with the beginning of the season and the renewed social whirl on Capri. The moment is much anticipated, for the simple reason that her home is like one huge living room filled by a circle of friends who share a an immense fondness for both her and Capri. Villa Narcissus is located in the island's medieval quarter just a few steps from the Piazzetta.

The dwelling conserves the flavour, atmosphere and almost oriental privacy reminiscent of Islamic cities, being surrounded by towering walls that conceal an evocative inner patio. The house has a long history of offering hospitality. Early on, it was used as guest quarters by the Convent of Suor Serafina. Later, in 1870, it was purchased by American painter Charles Coleman, who also used it to give hospitality to his painter friends, among them John Singer Sargent. It is said that Coleman bought it for the sole purpose of safeguarding a magnificent oleander growing in the courtyard. The painter was responsible for superimposing a Moorish style on the original seventeenth-century structure. The current owner has not only conserved the villa's structure as she found it, but even the trees and plants, which include the old palm in the patio, wisteria and a grapevine huge with age.

The secret of the unfailing success of her evening entertainment stems from knowing how to create just the right mix of Italians and foreigners from the world of international culture, plus the fact that all of them, perhaps unconsciously, are charmed by the setting and exotic atmosphere that permeates the villa. The dinner parties always take place in the old dining room, which contains a long table that is festively laid for such occasions with an inviting buffet. A considerable number of small tables are distributed throughout the rooms on different levels, in addition to the terrace and even the patio. The outstanding cuisine and fine wines facilitate sparkling conversation. If there is a lone regret, it is that nights on Capri pass so swiftly.

Pasta al garum

Garum was a Lucullian sauce used by the ancient Romans, and is still produced by hand today in a few maritime villages, where for centuries the drippings of anchovies and other fish have been artfully blended with other flavours. To complete a unique pasta seasoning, add sweet peppers or capers, olives, pine-kernels, sultana raisins, broccoli or other ingredients as desired, never forgetting to include a tiny amount of honey to balance the tart flavour of the garum. Before serving, garnish with a generous amount of pennyroyal.

Il Capricorno

"For us, Capri has always represented a corner of paradise, removed from the rest of the world and suspended in a dimension of time that is absolute – the type of memory that re-emerges in the mythical light and colour of past splendour: that of the Emperor Tiberius, who had no less than seven residences built here, and all the artists of every age who found in Capri a home and source of inspiration."

With these carefully chosen words, Livio declares his love for the island.

"Capri," Antonina continues, "intoxicates us with the loud chirping of the cicadas, the screeching of the seagulls, the fragrance of the cluster-pines, the jasmine, the orange blossoms and … the salt air.

Here everything is magical, the harmonious product of nature's grandeur."

It is in this splendid setting that they love to entertain guests at the family home, a typical example of Capri architecture.

It was designed by Livio's father, Carlo Angelo Talamona, who is credited with building some of the island's most prestigious homes from the 1930s to the 1960s.

The story of this particular house is one of change. It stands on what was once a deconsecrated church, incorporated in a hotel project in the 1950s.

Today the surprisingly versatile building houses a gallery of modern and contemporary art, making it a stimulating place for international artists and collectors to meet and exchange views. "For us," Livio resumes, "hospitality represents a ritual in the true sense of the word. Every detail takes on importance. Everything from the flowers to the fragrance and background music contributes to creating a convivial atmosphere for our guests."

An aperitif obviously marks the beginning of the dinner.

Out on the verandah, amidst roses and bougainvillea, the guest today enjoys fried squash blossoms and an assortment of goat cheeses seasoned with herbs, enjoyed with a glass of Falanghina del Sannio.

Then we take our place at the table inside. Coloured plates and Baccarat glasses stand out against the white linen tablecloth.

"It pleases me that nothing hints at the courses that will be served," the lady of the house remarks.

"Our first course may be a very typical dish, such as *pennette alla 'aumm aumm,'* followed by a risotto with shrimp flavoured with lemon and champagne."

"As a second course, we may serve grilled anglerfish au gratin with Mediterranean side dishes, such as aubergine with garlic and mint, sweet and sour peppers, potatoes *alla curcuma* and tossed salad, all washed down with a Fiano di Avellino."

"Next, fresh fruit kebabs and watermelon. For dessert, almond and pine-kernel ice cream, and a typical Capri chocolate or lemon cake with a good Passito di Pantelleria."

Pennette alla 'aumm aumm' (4 servings)

2 aubergines, garlic, 1 hot pepper, 500 g tomatoes (preferably the small pachino variety), basil, mozzarella.

Wash, slice and fry aubergines. Separately sauté garlic, hot pepper and tomatoes; when half-cooked, add aubergines. Cook the pennette (noodles) al dente. Flavour with sauce, diced mozzarella and plenty of basil. Before serving, garnish the dish with two small fresh basil leaves ... and buon appetito!

La Torre

Graziella Lonardi Buontempo, the driving force behind the "Premio Malaparte" literary prize organisation, has a way of entertaining guests that is anything but routine.

Her approach reflects her personality, which is instinctive and emphatic. What seems to guide her is the setting and company at any given moment. Capri may have its rules, but for her they are nothing more than cues.

La Torre has enjoyed the privilege of having Alberto Moravia as a guest for morning coffee in the shade of a wisteria, overlooking a stormy sea or inside out of a tedious drizzle. But starting the day in the company of a literary person is always stupendous.

"Hospitality is a very personal matter," says Graziella in her self-assured, unique manner. "For instance, I like to entertain barefoot." Even a simple luncheon, referred to as una colazione rubata, has its charms, such as a combination of mozzarella, tomatoes and freselle. The simplicity can be supplemented with something unexpected, such as a good chilled wine or coffee, or some other suitable find. The evening dinners are more elaborate. The tablecloth might be a colourful or plain one by Livio De Simone or one of plastic, raffia or cord, kind gifts from the artists with whom Graziella Lonardi collaborates on a regular basis. Strategic solutions are studied for the seating arrangements, menu and music on summer evenings when the moon is full. A dinner can be entirely red, meaning tomatoes, shrimp, lobster, red sweet peppers, watermelon and so on. Or all white: risotto, fish, cheeses, fennel, tropical salads with apples and white chicory. Or all green: pesto, French beans with mint, zucchini, salads and pistachio ice cream. "On such evening occasions," Graziella further elaborates, "I'm not fond of flowers of many colours. What I like is various types of grass and just a few white flowers, such as gardenias, camellias, tuberoses, calla lilies – in short, a combination of white and green, better yet if it is really fragrant. Centrepieces are definitely part of the table decoration, often made by artist guests. They may be made using grapes at harvest time, or artichokes and peppers or some other fruit."

On Capri it is possible to organise a real pizzeria outdoors, complete with a pizza chef, hat and all, something which has been done a number of times in connection with the Premio Malaparte. On such occasions, guests are treated to pizza, *pizzette, calzoni fritti* and *orecchiette* with tomato sauce, all served piping hot. Also available are anchovies with *fiorilli*. An oysterman

serves all the fresh oysters one could desire. The favourite recipes at La Torre involve tried and true first course dishes. Sometimes, though, recipes are created on the spur of the moment, like a painter choosing from his palette. At the seashore in the evening, preoccupation with weight watching tends to ease, if not slip away entirely. While pasta, salad and sweets can be arranged in endless combinations, the wines of the Campania region are a permanent feature. It never is out of style to serve the excellent local wines: Falanghina, Greco di Tufa and Gragnano.

Il Canile

With his gentlemanly charm, Dino Trappetti is among the leading figures in the social, cultural and artistic life of Capri.

"When I land on Capri," Dino says, "and begin to climb the stairs on my way home and see the cliffs, then I leave all the cares of the city behind me. Here at home the life I lead is without frills, but with the enormous luxury of the slow, easygoing pace of the islanders."

"It isn't so much the idea of a house at the seashore at any price, as having a home where you can watch the hibiscus bloom, or a gardenia – any white flower. Now that is something I never cease to admire." The house revolves around two bedrooms and a spacious living room with the typical cross vaults of Capri. The terraces are overflowing with maidenhair, cyclamens, lemons and hibiscus of different colours. Some of the grafting is most unusual. Practically anywhere one looks it is possible to admire orchids, violets and freesias, but also memorabilia and sculptures of Dalmatians. "For years, Il Canile (literally, the kennel) represented true relaxation for both Umberto and myself." Dino is the heir to and head of the famous Sartoria Teatrale Romana, the tailoring and dressmaking shop for the theatre founded by Umberto Tirelli. The ties of friendship binding the owners were strong: Umberto Tirelli, Lucia Bosé, Livio De Simone and Dino Trappetti lived together from 1969 to 1983. It was a house of friends for friends, where the numerous guests were always welcome. Dino learned long ago that, on this pleasure island, living in the open air is an art. His house is most pleasant inside and out. Dinner invitations here are much sought after, the dinners themselves enviable, the cuisine choice. In short, evening gatherings at Il Canile are as special as Dino Trappetti's lifestyle.

The appetisers prepared by Angela are exquisitely representative of the authentic cuisine of Capri: fried squash blossoms,

croquettes, aubergine with parmesan, fresh *caciotta* cheese. Equally unforgettable is the baba au rhum and chilled white wine, accompanied by all the latest gossip … and the moon over Capri.

Sformato di melanzane

Place mezze penne *noodles and fresh tomato sauce with mozzarella and meatballs, well garnished with basil, in a deep ovenproof dish. Cover with aubergine slices flavoured with mushrooms. Bake for 20 minutes, then turn upside down to form an aubergine-covered dome.*

Polpette

1 kg aubergines flavoured with mushrooms and combined with milk-soaked bread, 3 eggs, 200 g parmesan, 200 g pecorino cheese. Shape into olive-size rissoles, bread and fry.

Polpette di vitello o pollo

Grate 2 lemons and nutmeg over ground veal or chicken. Mix and shape into small rissoles. Place on a pan with a little olive oil and an unskinned garlic clove. Bake at high temperature for 20 minutes.

La Perla di Tragara

The house, which stands amid pines on the terraced land extending from Tragara in the direction of Tuoro, was designed and built in the 1930s by Carlo Angelo Talamona, the architect who, together with Edwin Cerio, created the style characteristic of the modern homes of Capri. The interior furnishings typical of the time have been preserved, further embellished by the bronzes and other objects collected over the years by the current owners, Flaminia and Mario Sonnino Sorisio. They make it a practice to leave Rome on weekends to enjoy family life here, which includes a common passion for the sea and sailing. Because of its position, La Perla di Tragara is a sort of country house at the seashore.

"Capri is a kind of hereditary disease," one of them adds, "that by now we've also spread to our children."

Flaminia takes pleasure in entertaining friends on the spacious terrace, whose salient feature is a beautiful well. The food is as refined as it is plain; the wines excellent. It is an ideal situation for frank conversation, amusing and serious by turns.

Gattò di patate (a Neapolitan dish sometimes made from leftovers)

8 servings: 2 kg potatoes, 7 eggs, 200 g mortadella, 200 g cooked ham, 200 g Parmesan, 2 mozzarella balls, 100 g butter.

Mash boiled potatoes while still hot, mixing in all the other ingredients, which have been diced. Add salt and pepper. Butter an ovenproof dish and sprinkle with breadcrumbs. Place the mixture in the dish and cover with breadcrumbs. Preheat oven to 180–200 °C and bake for 40 minutes. May be served cold the next day.

Polpette al limone

Add mashed potatoes and grated lemon rind to meatball mix. Combine and bread. Place meatballs in heated skillet with olive oil.

Impanatine

Make rissole mix using bread soaked in water. Firmly press each amount into the breadcrumbs until flattened to the shape of little Milan-style veal cutlets. Fry.

Il Southwind

*H*ospitality is an ingrained habit with the people of Capri after thousands of years of practising it. Here care is lavished on guests, to the point that even a visitor soon feels like an old friend.

The Cacace family has certainly done its part in honouring the tradition. In fact, for more than a century now it has made the receiving of guests in the grand style a philosophy of life.

The *South Wind* is a splendid 20-metre sailboat that Tonino Cacace makes available to his guests. Let us leave it up to one of them to describe life aboard her.

"On this splendid craft, the day begins at the tiny tourist port of Marina Grande. The captain, Massimo, and his second-in-command, Piero, distribute cocktails as a welcoming gesture. The atmosphere is pleasantly informal. Soon we set sail, and it is not long before we rediscover the island viewed from a spot that affords its most striking view – out to sea.

The *South Wind* dances on the waves; Capri, like a Siren of myth, enchants us with its landscape. We sail among bays and coves, listening to the crew's fascinating tales and amusing anecdotes. Then the aroma of freshly brewed coffee, soon to be served in delicate cups, reminds us that the time has come for a snack.

At lunchtime, the captain decides to drop anchor in a sheltered spot while Piero begins setting the table. On this occasion, too, the elegant service and *mise en place* are impeccable. The tablecloth is organdy, the cutlery is silver and the dinnerware is Capodimonte. Fittingly, today's menu is a homage to the cuisine of the Campania region and its genuine, hearty fare. It begins with mozzarella made from buffalo milk, tomatoes and basil, then proceeds to spaghetti with a

sauce of mussels and especially tasty hill tomatoes. Ginger ice cream splendidly tops off the meal.

The sharp cries of seagulls suddenly remind us of where we are. Weighing anchor, the captain points the prow in the direction of the Amalfi coast, and off we go.

Once there, we stop to take a dip in the crystal clear waters of the Bay of Nerano before landing to visit narrow streets lined with the sometimes pungent, always colourful shops of local craftsmen. Another surprise awaits us back at the boat. Once again, the table has been set with consummate skill, including seashells and crystal. Candles placed on the bridge flicker in the gathering dusk, their vanilla scent filling the air. The delicious main course is fish baked in lemon leaves. Now the stars are shining and a thousand coloured lights brighten the coastline. The evening will not soon be forgotten. After supper a toast is offered, then we set sail for Capri. On the approach, the cliffs are washed in moonlight. We correct ourselves: this night will never be forgotten.

The next day we wake up in the Bay of Marina Piccola. Breakfast is waiting: croissants, coffee, fresh lemon and orange juice, and that famous cake of Capri, hot out of the oven. If this isn't paradise … "

Il Coconut

Il Coconut is an expression of sun, sea and the pleasures of summer. The name in itself suggests the Caribbean, palms and good cheer. The original inspiration came from observing the launches that take tourists to visit the Blue Grotto. The next step was the handcrafting of a prototype in Sorrento.

The basic idea of the design was to incorporate enough size and stability to accommodate a group of friends and while away carefree hours with swims and fishing expeditions in the sparkling waters off Capri, Sorrento and Positano.

Among the snacks served on board is simple but delicious *pomodoro all'ostrica*, which is nothing more than a sun-ripened tomato cut in half and seasoned with just salt and lemon.

Another favourite is *panino di Aldo*, a sandwich made with sliced Sorrento tomatoes and well seasoned with plenty of olive oil, salt, basil and oregano. It is served in combination with mozzarella.

Another speciality not to be overlooked is *frittata di scammara*, made from spaghetti seasoned with a sauté of garlic, olive oil, black olives and hot pepper, with added breadcrumbs.

The bite-size fritters are normally eaten with the fingers.

Meals can be washed down with white wines from the Veneto or Campania regions. Naturally, the wines are always well chilled. An alternative beverage is *Sciantosa*, consisting of white wine, tonic water, sliced peaches and a pinch of sugar. Served in a carafe.

La casa della Canzone del Mare

"The first time I set foot on Capri," relates Fiona Winter Swarovski, "I arrived on a yacht. I disembarked at the Faraglioni and walked all the way up to the top of Via Tragara. Like countless others, I said to myself, 'This is where I want to live someday.'" But if her first husband was not particularly fond of Capri, she was fated to meet the man who would become her second husband right on that very island. "Years after that first visit, I came back to Capri with two of my friends. We were supposed to meet a Portuguese acquaintance of ours, who broke the appointment. But in his place he sent a Neapolitan prince … "

Today Fiona lives in the villa above Marina Piccola that once belonged to Gracie Fields. The house is set in a large garden with luxuriant vegetation. In its own way, the garden unfolds as spectacularly as a fireworks show. The Faraglioni stand out in the background as though in a painting, affording one of the best-loved views anywhere in the world. As for Fiona, in addition to being a designer and interior decorator, she is a beautiful woman with a disarming immediacy. Flamboyant and free of prejudices, she lives a pleasantly disorganised life surrounded by visiting children, dogs and flowers. Being drawn to beauty, she has left her special mark on the house, characteristically following her natural instincts. "I actually prefer Capri out of season," she goes on to say, "except in the springtime, when it rains incessantly. I have a great many acquaintances, but my happiest moments are when I'm with my three children, Arturo, Nicolas and Tajla. I love having guests over several times a week. The parties I put on in the garden are really quite grand." Those who have the privilege of being among the invited know just how refined the cuisine and wines are. A love for beautiful things and an innate sense of colour find joyful expression in the sumptuous table she sets, adorned with ceramics, coral, porcelain, crystal glassware and silver candlesticks.

Fiori di zucca

Squash blossoms, flour, brewer's yeast, salt.

Dissolve the brewer's yeast in a cup of lukewarm water and add flour. Add additional water as needed. Stir by hand for about 10 minutes until batter becomes smooth. Cover with a cloth and let stand for another 30 minutes. Dip blossoms in batter one at a time and deep fry in vegetable oil. Salt just before serving.

Torta ricotta e limone

Short pastry: 500 g flour, 300 g sugar, 200 g lard, 3 eggs, 1 packet vanillin. Filling: 500 g ricotta, 150 g sugar, 250 g crème patissière, 1 grated lemon.

Beat ricotta and sugar, add crème and grated lemon peel. Knead the short pastry and place on tin. Fill and cover with a top layer of short pastry. Bake at 180 °C for about 30 minutes.

Casa Tirrena

"My relationship with Capri is longstanding. You might call it a love affair that had a beginning but not an end." This is the way Wanda Ferragamo describes her strong ties to the island. "My fondest memory," she goes on, "was the time when Salvatore and I stayed here on our honeymoon. We put up at the Quisisana for five days, where we were immediately taken by the garden and the terrace covered with bougainvillea."

Her account continues, filled with memories and emotion. "Even afterwards, Salvatore and I used to come back to Capri every once in a while. We would pick the quieter time of year, and it was a pleasure to renew old memories. More than once we thought of buying a house on Capri, but always put off a decision.

At the time, of course, we wouldn't have been able to enjoy it to the full because Salvatore was pretty much on his own in the business and therefore always very busy."

"When I found myself alone with my children grown, I came to realise that a person who spends the holidays on Capri never feels like an outsider because the whole island is alive and enters into a friendly dialogue with those who visit it."

"In the course of another sojourn on Capri I also came to understand just how warm the reception of many vacationing Neapolitan ladies is. That was exactly the time when I finally decided to buy. I got in touch with a real estate agent, who showed me a great many houses before finally bringing me to Casa Tirrena, which I snapped up. It's a typical Capri home with vaulted ceilings, built by D'Amico, the shipowner.

That first day, when the doors leading to terrace opened, tears came to my eyes at the sight of so much beauty.

I didn't want to let on, but inside me a voice kept repeating that this was meant to be my holiday home."

"More than thirty years have passed since then, and every time I come to Capri I spend serene days in the company of friends who call on me. Lately, my three granddaughters – Vivia, Angelica and Consolata – also have been coming to visit. They adore Capri because here they feel free and easy."

"When the weather is too hot I prefer to stay at home reading or listening to good music on the terrace, which is very beautiful. There are always other times for the seashore."

"I am familiar with many resorts all over the world," she concludes, "but I have never encountered the magic of Capri, just as it is, anywhere else. Ever."

When it comes to giving dinner parties, Wanda Ferragamo prefers a menu with plain but tasty fare, including such classics as spaghetti with mussels or tomatoes stuffed with rice. Occasionally, the choice may fall on a cold rice dish with chunks of cantaloupe and a spoonful of mayonnaise, naturally accompanied by a chilled white wine.

La casa dei Russi

At the turn of the twentieth century, Capri was frequented by exiles, such as Maxim Gorky and his coterie of artists and intellectuals. Among the exiles was Ernesto Krunberg, born in Riga to an aristocratic Swedish family, who spent his student years in St Petersburg studying design. He came to Capri in 1913, where he remained for the rest of his life. What kept him there was a fateful encounter with a beautiful 16-year-old Russian girl, Tsera Solovieck.

His marriage with Tsera resulted in the birth in 1921 of two daughters, Mira and Juli. It was 'artist' Krunberg's desire to dedicate to them his lifelong dream home perched on the rocks overlooking Marina Piccola. Construction began in the late 1930s. It proved to be a long and laborious undertaking worthy of the "Fabbrica di San Pietro" (or, more to the point, that of St Petersburg). Krunberg himself designed the project, which explains the encounter/clash of Mediterranean and Nordic cultural influences. The current lady of the house enjoys having people over. Her style, at once simple and refined, reflects the villa's atmosphere. She has kindly given us one of her favourite recipes, as follows.

Involtini di melanzane

Large sweet peppers, aubergines al funghetto, olives, capers, a small amount of olive oil and anchovy pieces.

Roast and skin peppers, cutting them into long strips. Blend all the other ingredients to make the filling. Place a teaspoon of filling on each pepper strip, roll and place on baking tin with a little olive oil.

Bake at high temperature for 30 minutes.

La Piccola

"Capri joins and reunites its guests through the magic of its natural beauty. Capri's hospitality offers serenity, vigour and emotion." This is the opening statement by Giovanna Gentile Ferragamo. Her mother was the one who purchased the villa, being fascinated by its location in a natural amphitheatre with Monte Solaro in the background. Adding to the fascination was the villa's vast garden overflowing with jasmine, hibiscus and bougainvillea. The view overlooking the sea makes the rocky outcroppings even more majestic. "Every time I set foot in the house I am filled with joy," says Giovanna. Wife of Giovanni Gentile and mother of four, she is a cultivated, witty lady with a reassuring style. Her idea of a perfect day on Capri is to rise early and go boating for as long as she can under the sunny blue Mediterranean skies. In the evening she prefers to relax on the terrace of her home together with family and friends beneath starry skies, enjoying a simple meal and glass of good wine. "And laughing, joking and chatting," adds Giovanna, "until, before we know it, the day has slipped away and another is about to begin."

Zuppa rossa piccante (4 servings)

1.5 kg ripe tomatoes, 200 g carrots, 200 g celery, 200 g onions, 400 g potatoes, 1 yellow pepper.

Cut vegetables into fairly large pieces (except for the pepper) and place in a casserole with half a litre of water and a pinch of salt. Bring to a boil, cover and cook for 30 minutes. Run through blender, salt and add a pinch of hot pepper. Place chopped basil, a pinch of oregano, salt, hot pepper and 3 tablespoons of olive oil in a bowl and stir. Pour a very small amount of olive oil on soup and serve in soup plates garnished with diced yellow pepper and basil leaves. Spread small pieces of toast with basil sauce and serve with the cold soup.

La casa
sotto il Solaro

"In order to get to my house, I have to climb 150 sturdy country steps … But when I finally reach the top, it's as though my house wanted to repay me for my efforts."

This is how Raffaele La Capria describes his home in his *Capri e non più Capri*, published by La Conchiglia.

And he adds: "When, after two hours by train from Rome and an hour by hydrofoil, I reach the top, all at once I feel like I've flown in space and time into a world of water and rock still in a primeval state."

For years now, the famous essayist and writer has made this place, perched on a cliff falling straight down to the sea, his summer retreat.

This corner of Capri, located below rocky Monte Solaro and above the sea, affords a spectacular view of the Faraglioni. It seems light years away from the lively and worldly Piazzetta.

Those who live here will tell you in no uncertain terms that the place requires nothing more than simplicity, much as the surrounding nature.

There is something about the house that puts one in mind of the scene with the mystic oriental temple in the film *Razor's Edge*: it is an earthly paradise, but you have to suffer to get there.

Antonio and Piera are two free spirits whose way of entertaining is also inspired by simplicity and cordiality.

The best moment for them is in the evening, a time that allows them to enjoy the company of their friends far into the night.

In the matter of table decorations, they are partial to puppets and ceramic cake and fruit stands exclusively from Anacapri, as well as flowers from the garden that never fail to delight the senses.

But if the island offers all any hostess could ask for in terms of the setting, when it comes to cuisine this particular hostess prefers mixing traditional Tuscan recipes with local ones. In fact, this *métissage* is one of the secrets of her success, typified by her risotto with tomato sauce or *san marzano* (pear) tomatoes au gratin.

While waiting for the last guests to arrive, she likes to serve crostini with butter and anchovies along with the aperitifs. The anchovies should be boned and minced after rinsing away the salt.

Soften butter by working it with a wooden spatula. Add anchovies and continue working the butter until the anchovies are combined.

Risotto alla pomarola

Boil 2 heaped cups of rice for just a few minutes. Prepare the tomato sauce using tomatoes, 1 carrot, 1 onion and plenty of basil. Cook for 20 minutes, then strain. Add rice to sauce and continue cooking, adding broth until rice is thoroughly cooked. Serve topped with pieces of mozzarella and basil.

Linguine alla finta carbonara

Sauté bacon in skillet with a little olive oil, adding a dash of wine.

When pasta is cooked al dente, place in pan and continue to cook.

Add a handful of chopped basil just before serving.

Pomodori gratinati

Cut pear tomatoes in half lengthways, remove pulp and put through strainer. Add breadcrumbs, capers, anchovies, oregano, olive oil, salt and pepper. Chop the mixture, stuff the tomato halves and sprinkle with breadcrumbs. Bake for 15 minutes.

Budino di semolino

1 litre milk, 200 g sugar, lemon peel, 100 g semolina, 4 egg yolks.

Cook semolina for 20 minutes in milk with sugar and lemon peel; when lukewarm, add egg yolks.

Pour into a pudding mould lined with caramel and cook for 40 minutes in a double boiler.

Semifreddo al limoncello (8 servings)

2 extra fresh eggs, 175 g sugar, 250 ml milk, 10 g flour, 2 shots limoncello, lemon peel and juice, 500 g whipping cream.

Filling: place two lemon peels in milk in a small pan over a low flame. Mix flour with 75 g sugar and egg yolks in a bowl. At high temperature slice lemon peel and add part of mixture. Stir well before adding the remainder. Pour into the small pan over a low flame and stir again until obtaining a soft creme.

Meringue: in a double boiler, beat egg whites together with remaining sugar until firm. Add grated peel from remainder of lemon, limoncello and lemon juice to creme. Whip the cream. Gradually combine filling and meringue, then gradually add the mixture to the whipped cream. Line 8 individual moulds with plastic wrap.

Pour mixture into moulds. Tap each mould against a hard surface to eliminate any air bubbles.

Place moulds in freezer for at least 2–3 hours. Remove from moulds and place on individual plates.

Decorate with strawberry or chocolate sauce.

Crostata di marmellata (8 servings)

Short pastry: 240 g butter, 240 g sugar, 150 g eggs, 600 g cake flour, grated lemon peel.

Mix sugar and butter. Add eggs, grated lemon peel and flour in that order to obtain a consistent mixture.

Roll out the dough and place into pan. Spread uniformly with 1 cm apricot (or other) jam.

Bake at 180 °C for 45 minutes.

Caesar Augustus

The villa is located on Anacapri, perched on a marvellous rocky spur. The view of blue sea and sky is unsurpassed. "The feeling I hope to communicate," begins Paolo Signorini, "is that of the hospitality of a 'mountain villa at the seashore.' The style must be distinguished and soignée."

"Therefore," he continues, "in order to provide that sort of hospitality at the Caesar Augustus, I took my own home as a model for inspiration. And my home offers a brand of hospitality that communicates the fact that I like having people over: warmth, courtesy, great involvement … and all the rest, because my friends deserve this and more. At the Caesar Augustus there is never a moment when the guests feel anything but at ease, just like at home. This is as true on the terrace for an aperitif at sunset under the spell of the scenery, as at poolside for dinner by candlelight. The table decor is a careful *mélange* of refinement and elegance worthy of an exclusive residence." He further elaborates: "The attention to detail, the warm colours of the fabrics and the decorations of the ceramics are what I have chosen as a sort of underlying motif. I want to stress the close connection between the physical plant and surrounding natural setting. This is a real must, no less than a bouquet of flowers fresh from the garden."

The same intense approach applies to the cuisine, which features simple traditional Mediterranean dishes accompanied by exquisite regional wines. "My real secret?" Signorini concludes. "Two passionate cooks, Gianna and Pasquale, who use the best pure ingredients, starting with tomatoes fresh off the vine from the terraced kitchen-garden below the swimming pool." For the first time ever, he reveals two recipes meant as a tribute to Anacapri.

Scialatielli dell'isola di sopra

Pasta (*scialatielli*, a special semi-dry home-made type, is ideal), garlic, extra virgin olive oil, 1 hot pepper, very fresh boned anchovies, green olives, freshly grated lemon rind, salt, parsley.

Sauté small pieces of garlic in a large skillet with olive oil. Add hot pepper, taking care not to cause the olive oil to smoke. Delicately place a few boned anchovies side by side on the sauté, cover and cook for no more than 2 minutes. Uncover and add large chunks of green olives, finely chopped parsley and grated lemon before salting. Drain the scialatielli and carefully combine with the sauce, trying to keep the anchovies whole. Garnish with small parsley leaves.

Linguine alle erbe e ai profumi dell'isola felice

Sauté a small amount of chopped garlic in olive oil. Add hot pepper, a small handful of minced salted capers, immediately followed

by a few halved tomatoes (the pachino *variety is recommended).*

Season with fresh marjoram, salt to taste and thicken by adding a small handful of finely chopped almonds.

Cook for 1 minute.

Add linguine cooked al dente to the sauce.

Top with a good amount of basil leaves and a few black olives cut into chunks.

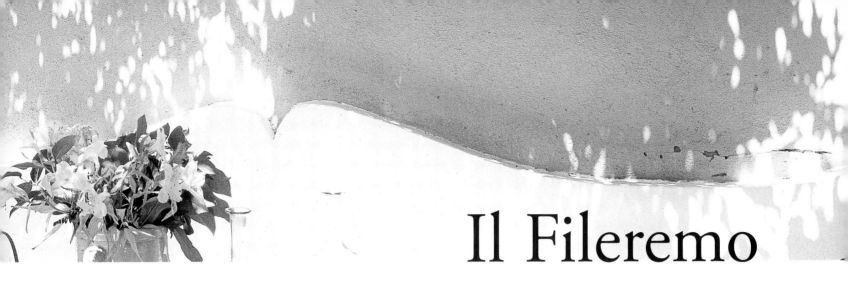

Il Fileremo

Gabriella Feletti is the brilliant lady of the house known as "Il Fileremo." Together with her brother Gianmario, she favours a decidedly informal style when it comes to entertaining. The house itself lends itself to this approach, having a layout that allows guests total independence to enjoy what the island has to offer.

The appointed hours for getting together are naturally dinner and suppertime, perfect occasions for discussing an excursion, swim or encounter at one of the cafés on the Piazzetta.

"I can't conceive of my home without guests," Gabriella says. "It would be a waste. Sometimes our friends drop in when we're away. I really am very fond of my house. I care for it, I pamper it. When I have to depart I say goodbye and a lump comes into my throat – and, in my opinion, the feeling is mutual. That's why I'm always glad not to leave it all by itself, so that someone is here to experience it and enjoy the flowers and panoramas."

Gabriella is one who cooks a lot, especially for guests. Her secret is to alternate the cuisine of Milan and Piedmont, where she has her roots, with that of Capri and Naples, her adopted homes.

This explains why on the table we find crêpes with fontina, and cooked ham with mushroom sauce, as well as lukewarm minestrone with a tablespoon of pesto, crispy cutlets and aubergine rissoles, roulades stuffed with raisons and pine-kernels stewed in fresh tomatoes and, finally, *gattò*, her version of the potato dish that Neapolitan friends claim surpasses the *gattò* their grandmothers used to make.

When it comes to dessert, the compass needle decidedly swings north. The most popular sweets include small vanilla-flavoured soufflés topped with melted dark chocolate, and *tarte tatin* right out of the oven, with a side dish of crème Chantilly and apricot strudel.

"As for wines," Gabriella Feletti concludes, "I leave that to my brother Gianmario. Another of his tasks is the seating arrangement, which it is most important to do properly, since easy conversation is a primary ingredient for any successful dinner party."

Crêpes alla Fileremo

100 g cooked ham, 100 g mild fontina, 20 g dried mushrooms, 1 garlic clove, approximately 20 g butter, 30 g parmesan.

Soak mushrooms in lukewarm water for 20 minutes, then drain while reserving water. Cook mushrooms together with garlic and butter for 20 minutes. Filter and add reserved water as needed to prevent mushrooms from drying out.

Take care that some liquid remains. Add salt and pepper. Stuff the crêpes with ham and fontina chopped into fair-size chunks and combine with half of the previously prepared béchamel.

Arrange the crêpes in a single layer in a buttered ovenproof dish. Chop the mushrooms into fairly large pieces, mix with the remaining béchamel and spread the mixture on the crêpes. Sprinkle with parmesan.

Bake in a pre-heated oven at 190 °C for 15 minutes. Brown by placing under grill for 3 or 4 minutes after removing from oven.

Casa Colette

Walking through the centre of Anacapri, if one leaves behind the Church of San Michele with its stupendous eighteenth-century ceramic tile floor and heads in the direction of I Traversa Timpone, it is impossible to miss Casa Colette or, as the old-timers call it, the *casa d'a francesa*. Here, in fact, is where the French writer purchased various residences from the locals, which she remodelled in keeping with the style of the island. Originally, the entire property belonged to the friars of the Church of San Michele and was used by them as a monastery. Once past the black gate, one enters a short, whitewashed passage with a barrel vault that leads into a central patio with an eighteenth-century well. The patio in turn opens onto the pergola of the garden – a true *hortus conclusus* with high walls on all sides and columned pathways covered by grapevines. The masonry structure of the pergola has a whitewash finish. The use of white continues inside, brightening the whole interior. Outdoor life in Capri generally leads to interior decoration that reflects the exterior of the dwelling, with terraces typically forming a vital part of a house's soul. Mediterranean taste definitely is partial to houses facing the sea, or else luxuriant hanging gardens where domestic life continues unabated out in the sunshine or the shade of a pergola. In Casa Colette, the terraces are arranged on various levels; large and small stairways enliven the architecture. The interior ceilings have characteristic cross and ribbed vaults. Panels of *azulejos* decorate the walls of the garden, which also has marble basins and statues from Signa, and is paved in the typical Capri way using pebbles from the beach. The house is both sophisticated in taste and welcoming. The sparse furnishings include a few antiques and some typical majolica pieces coloured manganese, yellow and blue, which lend a special touch. The house reflects the fact that it is occupied summer and winter by Dinella Vitale, a strong-willed woman with a vital personality very much anchored in the present. Her frank opinions are sometimes surprising, always stimulating, never lacking in humour. Whether her houseguests are her visiting children or friends, Dinella's naturally hospitable ways are evident even early in the morning. Her breakfasts are hearty, featuring croissants to suit every taste, including creme, chocolate and jam fillings and Neapolitan style. Homemade jams are another item, in addition to fresh orange juice squeezed from oranges picked outside in the garden. Breakfast is served on a table spread with a lovely tablecloth. A vase of fresh flowers is never missing. The style of Casa Colette combines sophistication, simplicity and ease. With such a demanding, polished hostess it could hardly be otherwise.

Ziti renversè

400 g ziti (or some other large noodle), 1 kg canned peeled tomatoes, garlic, olive oil, chopped parsley, hot pepper.

Sauté 3 garlic cloves in a skillet with a little olive oil and hot pepper. When garlic is thoroughly browned, add peeled tomatoes and cook for 30 minutes. Break ziti by hand, partially cook in boiling water, drain and pour into skillet. Flavour for 10 minutes. Sprinkle with chopped parsley and serve. My husband, the inventor of the dish, named it ziti renversè because instead of putting the sauce on the pasta, the procedure is reversed.

Spaghetti alle vongole

400 g spaghetti, 500 g canned peeled tomatoes, 1 kg clams, 1 bouillon cube, garlic, olive oil, hot pepper, chopped parsley.

Sauté the garlic and hot pepper in a deep skillet. When garlic is browned, add clams, cover immediately and cook for 5 minutes. When clams have opened, add peeled tomatoes and bouillon cube; cook for 10 or 15 minutes. Cook the spaghetti barely al dente, place in skillet, mix and serve with a sprinkling of parsley.

Crostata di tagliolini all'uovo

350 g thin tagliolini, mozzarella, béchamel, peas, 50 g prosciutto, grated parmesan.

Butter a 25 cm-diameter ovenproof pan and sprinkle with breadcrumbs. Cook pasta al dente; place half of cooked pasta in pan, pressing it down slightly with the fingers. Spread the pasta with béchamel and cover with sautéed peas, diced prosciutto and grated parmesan. Place the remaining pasta on top, press down with fingers and sprinkle with breadcrumbs. Bake for 30 minutes. Satisfaction is guaranteed.

La casa su Cala del Rio

By the time we reach the house, we are lost in reverie after taking the lovely walk that descends from Anacapri along the road leading to the Grotta Azzurra (Blue Grotto). Designed to fully exploit the natural setting of sea and sky, it is like a white brushstroke in the thick vegetation, with the aquamarine waters of Cala del Rio as a backdrop.

The relationship between nature and man is so intensely reciprocal as to suggest that the architectural design was created together with the landscape.

The original shape of the rooms and masterly counterpoint provided by glimpses of the panorama form an ideal entity in keeping with the indoor/outdoor lifestyle characteristic of Capri. The garden surrounding the house is full of trees, including tall pines, olives and fruit trees; the layout features flowerbeds, alleys and terracing, further embellished by nineteenth-century terracotta statues produced in Signa and a large neo-classic marble basin with hot and cold running water. The outside stairs are designed to circle around an ancient olive. The whitewashing has the effect of shaping the exterior into a graceful whole, including the curved walls of different heights and windowsills.

The bright sunny terraces are very much in the Mediterranean style, providing an ideal spot for entertaining guests. There one can relax on soft cushions placed on whitewashed masonry seats designed for the purpose. Each terrace is intended for a different use based on the exposure. It is a pleasure to be able to relax over a drink on the west terrace and enjoy the fiery sunset as the sky deepens and streaks with pink. At suppertime we shift over to the side with the vertical drop overlooking the sea.

The meal is served by candlelight under beach umbrellas.

When the weather suggests that it is better to stay indoors, the atmosphere is warm and intimate. The oval dining room is made even cosier by the Wedgwood china, including a soup tureen. A pair of windows is designed along the lines of eighteenth-century Neapolitan architecture; one faces the blue of the sea, the other the soothing green of the garden. The culture and personality of the homeowners is clearly evidenced in the layout and furnishings, with the latter being exclusively family heirlooms. The house has a lived-in feel, where old and new combine to create an atmosphere that reflects the best of yesterday and today. It is not just a summer place, but a real country home all year round. Any time of day, the place is awash in light and colour, adding to the spectacular surroundings.

Peperoni all'orientale (4 servings)

4 large sweet peppers of different colours, olive oil, salt, pine-kernels, sultana raisons, capers, black olives, breadcrumbs, garlic, parsley.

Grill whole peppers (taking care not to overcook). Remove skin and use scissors to cut into strips about 1 cm wide. Coat bottom of ovenproof dish with olive oil and add peppers. Add olive oil, salt, capers, pitted black olives, raisons previously soaked in water and squeezed by hand, pine-kernels, chopped garlic and parsley. Sprinkle with breadcrumbs mixed with chopped parsley and a small amount of olive oil. Bake in pre-heated oven at high temperature for approximately 10 minutes. Serve lukewarm.

Braciolette (4 servings)

300 g ground veal, bread with crust removed and soaked in milk, 100 g mortadella, 4 tablespoons dry white wine, sliced bread loaf, bay leaf, a few tablespoons of dry white wine, olive oil, 1 egg, 40 g parmesan, salt, pepper, 20 g butter, wooden skewers.

Pour wine over ground veal and allow to stand for a time before mixing with milk-soaked bread that has been thoroughly squeezed. Add egg, parmesan, salt and pepper. Shape into small oblong patties.

Remove crusts from sliced bread and cut each slice in two.

Skewer in order: a bay leaf, a piece of bread, a veal patty, a few strips of mortadella and another piece of bread. Repeat.

Place skewers in a pan coated with olive oil.

Add a flake or two of butter to each patty and slice of bread.

Bake in medium oven for about 20 minutes.

L'Approdo

The handsome 1967 villa stands on a panoramic road, Via di Palazzo a Mare. In designing it, architect Adinolfi took pains to respect Capri's typical style.

In the large central area, the design of the fine floor tiles by Stinco borrows from an old Capodimonte pattern.

A lovely skylight illuminates the flooring to good effect. The white ceiling has cross vaults.

The living room has a wonderful surprise in store for first-time guests: a picture window framing the Bay of Naples and Mt Vesuvius. A large hung painting by Novelli recalls the dominant themes of the house: the white of the interior and blue of the sea.

Although the lady of the house lives much of the year in Rome, her treasured roots are in Capri, where she returns whenever she can.

She has travelled widely, especially in the East; her affection for that part of the world is reflected in the decor of the villa with its many fascinating Oriental objects, including valuable Chinese furniture.

The villa's large garden abounds in luxuriant Mediterranean flora, such as bougainvillea, jasmine, hibiscus, oleander and lemons.

The villa is among the very few on the island fortunate enough to have a way down to the seaside on the property. And when it comes to a meal on the terrace or a picnic on the rocky shore, the fragrance of the flowers combined with the fresh salt air make for an unforgettably sublime experience.

Brioche napoletana (8 servings)

400 g flour, 180 g butter, 1 cake compressed yeast dissolved in a glass of milk, 4 egg yolks and 4 whites beaten until stiff,

a pinch of salt. Mix all the ingredients, preferably in an earthenware bowl.

Work dough by hand, starting in the middle. Keep throwing dough against side of bowl until it no longer sticks.

Butter a pan 10 cm high. Add the dough to the mould, cover, and allow to rise for 2 hours in a closed, cool place.

Bake at 70–80 °C for 15 minutes, then raise temperature to 150 °C and bake for an additional 15 minutes.

Serve hot after filling hole with béchamel and a vegetable: artichokes or mushrooms or French beans.

The dish is accompanied by a sauceboat containing béchamel and parmesan.

Riso alle erbe (8 servings)

600 g boiled white rice seasoned with olive oil, plenty of lemon, sage, mint, basil, marjoram and garden rocket.

Finely chop herbs; add olive oil and lemon.

Salt to taste and season boiled rice with the pesto, which must be sufficient to colour the rice green. Serve cold.

Riso al pesce

500 g white rice, 800 g grouper or dentex, mayonnaise, 3 lemons, olive oil, parsley.

Boil rice and season until green in colour with a plentiful sauce, as follows: 2 tablespoons mayonnaise, juice of 3 squeezed lemons, minced parsley, olive oil, salt.

Break part of fish into pieces in a separate bowl, then combine with rice.

Garnish with remainder of fish.

Spaghetti con vongole e zucchine (8 servings)

1 kg small clams, 300 g zucchini, 2 garlic cloves, extra virgin olive oil, parsley, hot pepper, 1 glass white wine,

salt, 1 kg spaghetti or linguine.

Place clams in a bowl of cold water.

Clean the zucchini, removing seeded middle portion before cutting into long thin strips.

Boil the spaghetti in salted water.

Sauté sliced garlic together with hot pepper in a large skillet. When garlic begins to brown, add well-drained clams

and cook for 2 to 3 minutes. Add a glass of white wine and the zucchini, covering skillet.

Cook until clams completely open. Add a good amount of chopped parsley and salt to taste.

Discard any unopened clams. Drain spaghetti when cooked and place in the skillet. Cook for another 1 or 2 minutes.

Serve piping hot.

Grotte Bleue

This nineteenth-century residence with the evocative name was originally one of the island's first hotels. From the terrace of the Grotte Bleue it seems almost possible to reach out and touch a panorama of breathtaking beauty.

Donna Vicky Romano née de Dalmases and her husband Valerio had the foresight to preserve the original paintings in the style of ancient Pompeii that adorn the walls of what was once the hotel dining room. These grotesques are the only ones remaining intact anywhere on Capri, representing a type of decoration in vogue in stylish homes here at the turn of the twentieth century. "I first came to Capri in 1978," recalls Vicky Romano. "I remember being struck by the scent of the flowers and the fantastic pink of the rocks. Not only that, I was taken with the history that I saw written in every tile, the completely special atmosphere. Afternoons I adored sitting in the Piazzetta, which was truly the place to be on Capri."

"Plus," she continues, "this is the island of romance. That same summer I met Valerio. I remember that we went to the 'Canzone del Mare,' where Peppino Di Capri was performing. It was a perfect evening, lit up by a huge bright Capri moon. Twenty-five years have passed since then and … we're still together."

"I adore our home on the port," she resumes, "for the sense of freedom and peace it gives me. The sight is brimming with life! In the morning I can observe the reawakening of the island, perhaps over breakfast with guests. It is a delight to find the table laid, while Salvatore, who is part of the family and a pillar of the home, entertains everyone with his amusing stories. In the late afternoon towards sunset the boats come in. The evening … is truly enchanting!"

The art of entertaining comes naturally to Vicky and Valerio Romano. They make good use of a large outdoor table to

organise dinners with twenty invited guests, but whose initial number may double within a few hours, in keeping with the informality typical of Capri social life. Local products play a leading role in the preparation of the menu. That means leaving plenty of room for vegetables, even for dishes that might seem inappropriate for the hot summer months, such as pasta with squash, which instead turns out to be refreshing. Capri-style ravioli with fresh tomatoes and plenty of basil is a steady favourite. "I like attending to the details," Vicky Romano confides. "I adore candles. I believe that suggestive lighting and background music that fits the occasion are two essential ingredients for creating an ideal atmosphere. Nature does the rest. It goes without saying that one thing I never do without is flamenco music, my real passion. I enjoy the simple things in life, the ones that come naturally. And, above all, I believe that for an evening to be successful the key is to entertain for the sheer pleasure of it, not just to return invitations. And, here on Capri, that is exactly what I do."

La Tiberiana

Sauté an onion, add prosciutto and allow to brown. Next add diced red and yellow sweet peppers. Leave covered for 30 minutes.

Season the pasta (preferably mezze penne) with plenty of fresh basil and grated parmesan.

Risotto al limone

This dish is practically identical to risotto alla milanese, the only difference being the grated lemon rind in place of saffron.

Top with cream and parmesan.

Lino Capri

Necessary qualities and helpful hints for home entertainment on Capri

You must trust in the Gods in the hope that the weather will be clement. If a garden party is involved, 'weather permitting' is a necessary proviso, since even a star-spangled evening can turn into a torrential downpour. In view of the island's intense social life, your invitations must go out well in advance or else you may discover that your friends have a previous engagement at the villa next door. If extending invitations takes a certain knack anywhere, it is all the more so on a tiny island. One's social antennae must be attuned to the nuances to avoid running the risk of a mismatched guest list.

Food and drink must be plentiful, among other things because guests often show up famished after walks around the island. Another reason is the local habit of bringing a friend or two along, sometimes with their spouses and relatives, including children, or even someone nice just met in the Piazzetta or fresh off the boat. As a result, you may find your house full of brilliant strangers. It is all but impossible to be a misanthrope on Capri.

Forget the idea of going to bed before dawn. Do not be surprised if in the social whirl you happen to discover a recycled gift of yours. Sometimes it requires forbearance to have to hear the same old stories again.

You must give clear directions to your home. Someone unfamiliar with where you live may wander around for hours on the byways before finding the right address … just as you are bidding the last of the other guests goodnight.

Take a real interest in your guests, using all your ability to make them feel at home. Merely opening a bottle of wine and lighting a few scented candles will not suffice to create the right atmosphere.

All that remains for me to do is wish you a pleasant evening.

Traditional Recipes

The savoury anecdote with which we introduce additional traditional recipes from Capri relates to the chocolate almond cake known as *torta caprese*. This sweet's origin is associated with the drawing room of two American ladies, Kate and Sadee Walcott Perry, who disembarked on the island in 1897. Famous for their Sunday afternoon tea parties attended by Anglo-American society, their tumultuous Sapphic passions became the target of the jibes of Compton Mackenzie. We leave it to the reader to imagine what role the cake played in all this.

Ravioli alla caprese (4 servings)

Pasta: 500 g flour, 1 tablespoon olive oil, hot water, salt. Filling: 500 g caciotta cheese, 3 eggs, 100 g parmesan, marjoram, salt, pepper (optional).

Heap flour in a ring, pour olive oil in centre well. Add water and knead until obtaining a soft, consistent dough, adding more flour as needed. Grate the caciotta into a bowl and combine with eggs, parmesan, a little marjoram and a pinch of salt, as well as pepper if desired. Work the filling.

Roll out the dough to form a rectangle. Place the filling on the sheet of dough in separate small amounts.

Cover with the remaining pasta. Use a tumbler to cut out the ravioli. Serve with a plain tomato sauce and sprinkling of parmesan.

Garnish with basil leaf.

Cavateddi provola e zucchine (4 servings)

400 g home-made cavateddi, butter, 1 white onion, zucchini, basil, pepper, meat sauce, tomatoes, smoked provola cheese, parmesan and salt.

Cut zucchini crosswise and fry. Sauté chopped onion in skillet with butter. Add fried zucchini, pepper, basil, a small amount of meat sauce and a few fresh tomatoes. Salt to taste.

Cook pasta, drain well and place in same skillet. Add diced smoked provola and parmesan. Stir as it cooks a bit more over high flame. Serve hot.

Linguine a modo mio (4 servings)

350 g linguine, garlic, olive oil, 4 or 5 small fresh tomatoes, 1 hot pepper, 4 prawns, 400 g shellfish, garden rocket.

Sauté garlic, olive oil and hot pepper. Add tomatoes and prawns. When the latter are partially cooked, add shellfish. Cook and drain linguine; invert on finished sauce. Stir as it cooks over high flame, adding a bit of chopped garden rocket.

Involtini di pesce spada (4 servings)

500 g swordfish, a few bay leaves, 12 small rectangles of smoked provola cheese, salt and pepper. Sauce: olive oil, garlic and lemon.

Cut swordfish into a dozen or so very thin slices. Place on flat surface. On each slice place a piece of bay leaf and small rectangle of smoked provola. Sprinkle with salt and pepper. Form a roll from each slice and barbecue. Season with sauce of garlic, olive oil and lemon. Each portion consists of three fish rolls arranged like spokes on the plate.

Cuoccio all'acqua pazza (2 servings)

1 sea robin (or gurnard) weighing 600 g, garlic, olive oil, 1 onion, white wine, 350 g fresh tomatoes.

Thoroughly wash and scale fish. Place olive oil, a whole garlic clove and the onion in a skillet to sauté. Place the whole fish in the skillet and add a dash of white wine. Allow wine to evaporate before adding fresh tomatoes. Cook over low heat. Serve with croutons.

Carpaccio con salsa ai porcini (4 servings)

500 g beef fillet, garden rocket, 200 g boletus mushrooms, pepper, salt, olive oil, lemon.

Meat: slice meat into thin slices and place on dish or platter covered with garden rocket.

Add pepper, salt, olive oil and lemon;

allow to stand for 10 minutes.

Sauce: cut mushrooms into thin slices and place in a bowl with olive oil, a whole garlic clove and the juice from 1 lemon.

Pour sauce over carpaccio and garnish with slivers of parmesan.

Torta caprese

250 g butter, 250 g sugar, 300 g chopped almonds, 200 g dark chocolate, 5 eggs, 1 packet of vanillin.

Whip previously softened butter for about 5 minutes.

Add sugar, eggs (one at a time), chopped almonds, chocolate (melted in a double boiler) and vanillin.

Butter and flour pan before placing and spreading mix.

Bake at 170 °C for about 45 minutes.

Baba' al rhum

Dough: 250 g type 0 American-style flour, 40 g sugar, 5 g salt, 75 g butter, 20 g brewer's yeast, 6 eggs.

Syrup: 2 L water, 800 g sugar, 1 glass of rum.

Combine all dough ingredients, adding eggs one at a time.

Mix for 15 minutes.

Allow dough to rise until it has doubled in size.

Place in greased tube pan and allow to rise further.

When dough is level with the top edge of pan,

bake in preheated oven at 190 °C for 30 minutes.

Pour syrup over cake.

Torta ricotta e limone

Short pastry: 500 g flour, 300 g sugar, 200 g lard, 1 small packet vanillin. Filling: 500 g ricotta, 150 g sugar, 250 g custard, 1 grated lemon rind.

Whip ricotta together with sugar. Add custard and grated lemon rind. Work the short pastry according to traditional methods, then use it to line baking tin before pouring the filling.

Cover with another layer of short pastry. Bake at 180 °C for about 30 minutes.

Pastiera napoletana

300 g ricotta, 300 g sugar, 300 g cooked wheat, 100 g diced candied fruit, 1 egg, 1 small packet vanillin, 10 drops millefiori (mixed honey) flavouring, short pastry.

Line a 20 cm-diameter pan with the short pastry. Separately beat the ricotta and sugar.

Add cooked wheat, candied fruit, egg and flavouring.

Place in pan. Cut strips of dough and weave lattice. Bake at 200 °C for about 1 hour.

Torta di mandorle caprese

250 g butter, 250 g sugar, 300 g ground almonds, 200 g melted dark chocolate, 250 g whole eggs, 50 g cocoa.

Combine butter and sugar. Add almonds, cocoa and chocolate melted in a double boiler. Finally, add the eggs. Bake at 200 °C for 45 minutes

Ricci capresi

Dip almonds cut lengthways in caramel and bake for about 1 hour until brittle. Heap in small amounts on a marble surface and cover with either melted dark chocolate or lemon-flavoured white chocolate.